Thou Shall Not Kill

What does God think about the killing of animals?

By
Kenneth Edward Barnes

Contents

Prologue

Today you see nature programs and television commercials about saving wildlife. Other times it is about animal cruelty. Some think that there should be no hunting or killing any animals at all. Others think there is nothing wrong with hunting, as long as you do not kill too many animals or rare and endangered ones. Then there are those that just see an animal as something they can exploit for profit.

Why am I writing this book? One reason is because since I can remember, I loved the outdoors and all the creatures that live in it. I'm also an outdoor writer and have been for many years. In addition to having outdoor news columns in local newspapers, I have written for several outdoor magazines, and I was a member of Hoosier Outdoor Writers for a long time where I won awards for my writing.

For a short time, I even worked at a local television station doing wildlife news segments. I have also hunted and fished since I was a child. And I'm a conservationist just as Theodore Roosevelt was. Many people do not think that these two can mix, but they can.

Besides having the insight of a hunter, angler and conservationist, I have also studied the Bible since I was fourteen-years-old. One of the topics that I've studied, is how God views the way we treat animals. The other topic is about what is predicted to happen to the world, not only concerning the animals, but also to us.

How do we know what is right from wrong? That might sound like a dumb or stupid question, but it really isn't. Since the beginning, man has decided what was good or evil and if you look at history, you will see that he has not always made the correct decisions. At times, all of us have made wrong decisions. Only until a hundred and fifty years ago, the people that owned and sold slaves felt they were in the right. Today there are other controversial topics or issues that people often argue and debate about, and one is the killing of animals.

Is it wrong to eat meat? Is it wrong to kill a wild animal? What about the abuse of an animal, and what is abuse? Does the commandment given by God, 'Thou shall not kill,' mean people, or does it also mean animals? Does God tell us how we are to treat animals in our care? This is the reason for this book.

I wanted to approach the subject of taking the lives of animals by giving a balanced view, but at the same time give the view of the one that created them.

Recently I wrote *Do Pets go to Heaven?* I have had some good feedback on this book as many have wondered if they will ever see their beloved pets again. What I say in that book may surprise you.

I also wrote a book called *Mysteries of the Bible*. It explains many things that people often wonder. What happens when you die? What day is God's Sabbath? Is evolution true? When was Christ born? When is the Lord returning to earth and many others.

Many years ago, my brother and I were discussing several things I believed that churches were doing contrary to the Scriptures. I challenged my youngest brother to prove me wrong. After studying Greek and Hebrew Scriptures for a few months, he found out that I was correct. He also discovered he wasn't following Christ as he should. He has since become a minister and now has his own congregation and an independent church.

This book will not be very long and I could probably tell the entire story in a long article. However, I believe it is an important issue for today and I would like to include a few stories from my newspaper and magazine articles along with a few excerpts from a couple of my other books. This way you can see and understand my feelings, as well as how I believe God views the killing of animals.

Many do not know, but the Bible is the first book that ever talks about conservation. In the Scriptures, God tells us how we are to treat the earth and its creatures. I hope by my words and His that I will be able to show you what He says about how we are to treat our fellow creatures, the creatures that share this tiny speck of dust in the universe with us.

Yes, in this short book of about 31,000 words, I believe I can answer the question that this book poses. What does God think about the killing of animals?

Chapter 1

In the Beginning

It would take much too long to write everything about the beginning of the world, as we know it, in this one chapter. That is why I have written *Mysteries of the Bible* and *Christ: His Words, His Life.* These two books go into more detail about how and why God made the world, especially *Mysteries of the Bible.* I explain that what many believe, or what they have heard, is not necessarily what the Bible actually says. The earth is far older than six thousand years and God says so in several places.

Therefore, I will not try to explain, in this book, the past before we were here as it is not important to the subject at hand. I will begin at the beginning, at least where most believe the beginning starts, and that is in the Garden of Eden.

In Genesis 1:30, God said that He had made every creature on earth to be only vegetarians. This was soon to change, and did, when Adam and Eve disobeyed God and listened to the "Father of Lies", the "advisory", the one most know as Satan.

After the fall of man, God slew two animals and "clothed" Adam and Eve, who were our first parents. The Bible does not say what kind of animals He killed, but because of what happened later, you can be fairly certain that they were sheep. We also know that He probably killed two animals because it says He made *coats of skin*s for them both. It would take a large animal such as a cow to make two coats, but it is possible. That does not matter very much because the fact is that an animal had to die in order for them to be clothed.

Now blood was shed to "cover" their sin. Things then changed in the natural world and they are to stay this way for many centuries.

When mankind was first given the earth and before they had disobeyed, God told them to "subdue it" and have dominion over all the animals, Genesis 1:28. This has now happened. It took many centuries and many mistakes, but the earth has been brought under control by humans. Nature, however, does not like to be controlled and it will fight back. Man has not only subdued the world, he has damaged much of it in doing so. God, however, did not intend for this to happen. This is why He gave instructions on how to treat the earth and the animals that we share it with in His Word.

In Deuteronomy 20:19, God instructed the people of Israel not to cut down and destroy any trees that produced fruit or nuts that humans used as food. He told them this when they would be at war and even needed wood in the siege of a city. Today, many disregard what God wishes and destroy jungles, trees and land that would support people and animals.

We have cleared the land for farming, blocked the rivers with dams, turned swamps into housing developments, and changed the entire face of the earth.

Some of what we have done is good; much of it, however, is not. I will discuss more of this later.

In the beginning, the world was new and there were few of us. We did not have the means to change very much of our natural surroundings, therefore we lived alongside nature.

We were pretty much at the mercy of predators and the elements. It did not take long, however, that we began to fight back, to protect ourselves, and to do as God had said and subdue our world.

Before Noah, man had already built great cities and been able to grow all of the food that was needed, both plants and animals. Because of this, humans had plenty of idle time to think of other things. What they thought of, however, was how they could enjoy themselves at the expense of others. The world soon became a place of violence, bloodshed, and most likely the destruction of the natural world. Sounds just like today, doesn't it? This is also predicted in the Bible in Matthew 24:38 and in Luke 17:26.

What has this to do with how God views the killing of animals?

This book is called "Thou Shall Not Kill. What does God think about the killing of animals?" There are two sides to this question and that is the purpose of this book.

Chapter 2

The Early Days

In the early days of civilization, just as there are today, birds and animals were killed for food. Some were killed for their skins for clothing. Others were killed to protect the people's poultry, sheep or other livestock, and some were killed as pests.

During the first days of civilization, there were few people and most of the earth was covered with forests or other areas of natural habitat. In Europe, as well as the Middle East, there were brown bears and lions (the bear existed in the land of Israel until the early 1900s). The African lion was common in southern Spain, Greece, Italy, Turkey, and as far east as India. Today, only a few dozen lions are still in India. The leopard was also common in Africa, the Middle East, and all the way to India as was the cheetah, (the leopard was thought to be gone from the Middle East until a few were found living in the hills of Jordan in the 1960s). In India and many countries around it, the tiger roamed in the tens of thousands. Different subspecies of it even lived as far north as Siberia along with the Amour leopard.

Also, in Europe and Asia, wild boar made their home right beside countless packs of wolves that lived even down into Israel.

In North America, there were grizzly bears in the west all the way down into Mexico and the plains grizzly lived in the plains of the Dakotas and where Kansas would later be. There were also cougars over the entire continent as well as in South America. The jaguar likewise, made its home in South and Central America. Its range also extended as far north as Texas, Arizona, New Mexico and southern California. When America was first discovered there were even reports of it as far east as Florida, Tennessee and the Carolinas.

During these early days, wild animals were considered enemies and often were. In the days of the bubonic plague of Europe, there were stories of wolves coming out of the forests, running into homes, and taking babies from the arms of their mothers.

Shepherds of old, like those mentioned in the Bible, often had to defend their flocks from bears, wolves, lions, and leopards.

The pioneers in America also had to be on the constant lookout for bears, wolves, and mountain lions, which would often kill their livestock. The early settlers had to depend on maybe their one and only horse, ox or cow. They had to have a horse or ox to help clear and plow their land. They needed a cow that would provide milk, which was also used to make cheese and butter. Pigs roamed free in those days, but bears often preyed on them.

You can see why these predators were not well liked. Most of our ancestors barely scraped by and if something happened to an animal they depended on, they may not have survived.

It was man against the world. These predators created fear and for good reason. Not only could they destroy the animals that you and your family depended on for survival, they could kill you or any member of your family. There was also not much understanding about many of these animals and they were seen as "the enemy," and in many cases, they were.

It was not easy to defend yourself or your animals from large predators before firearms were invented. Dogs were domesticated and, in many places, used to help protect livestock and humans alike.

During the early days of civilization, predators were abundant as was wilderness. We were more or less at the mercy of a wild and cruel world. This was the mind set for nearly all people on the earth.

We did not have the power to destroy very many animals and it would be many centuries before our numbers increased enough to make much different in the world. But increase we did. We also invented more and better weapons, weapons to use to defend ourselves and weapons to kill large and dangerous animals.

Chapter 3

The Good, the Bad, the Ugly

Some animals were good. People depended on many wild animals for food and even shelter. The Native Americans used buffalo or bison hides for teepees, clothing and the rawhide to make bowstrings and cords. They used the bones for tools and arrowheads. Bison meat was the number one source of protein for the Plains tribes. Deer, likewise, was an important animal that not only the Native Americans depended upon, but also the early pioneers.

Animals such as bear, beaver, muskrat, wolverine, marten, fisher otter and others provided fur for warm clothing. It was said that Abraham Lincoln had a bearskin as a child while he lived in Indiana. (By the way, he lived at the other end of Little Pigeon Creek as a boy and young man. I was born on the banks of Little Pigeon Creek).

Many kinds of birds were also important to the native peoples as well as the early settlers. Flocks of *billions* of passenger pigeons migrated across the eastern half of North

America. Ducks, geese and swans filled the skies and covered the rivers and streams.

Sometimes, the enormous flocks of passenger pigeons would come to cropland and destroy everything in sight. At other times, when the crops failed, they were an important food supply.

In the early days of American settlement, the pioneers ate nearly everything and anything they shot or trapped. It did not matter if it was a muskrat, skunk, fox, lion, bear, possum, rabbit, squirrel or other kind of bird or animal. They could not run down to the corner grocery store, grab a package of meat and bring it home to put in the freezer. They had to depend on what they could raise or kill just to be able to survive. The same goes for the people of other lands in the days of their first settling there.

In the early days, there were plenty of birds and animals and few humans. We were at a disadvantage. America was a vast wilderness with wild animals roaming freely everywhere. I once read a story of a pack of wolves killing a man's horse in Warrick County, Indiana, in the 1840s. I was born in this same county only a little over one hundred years later.

I believe you can begin to understand the mind set of how people viewed animals in those days. Some were good, others bad and some very bad. How you viewed an animal often depended on the circumstance you were in at the time. Sometimes you needed them for food. At other times, the same animal destroyed your food. Therefore, the same animal could be good or bad.

In addition, in those days, people gave no thought about what the world would be like a hundred or two hundred years into the future. They had to worry about then and there and how to survive. There was no social security, no disability benefits, and no welfare checks in case things got bad.

This was one reason mountain men and explorers went west to trap and make money when the fur trade was booming. Market hunters also shot millions of ducks, geese, swans, and other birds to sell their meat or feathers. People did not think or care if the supply of birds or animals ran out, they only cared about how much money they could get from them. As abundant as many species were, most people never thought that they could all be killed and go extinct.

In the centuries preceding the invention of firearms, about the only way to catch or kill birds and animals were by traps or nets. Some were killed by bow and arrow or spear, and this was true for the Native Americans. In other countries, however, the poor usually did not have bows and usually did not take many animals from the wild.

In South America, the natives used blowguns with poison darts to take small birds, monkeys and other game and they still do. The aborigines of Australia used boomerangs to hunt their food. With the invention of firearms, things were to soon change.

Chapter 4

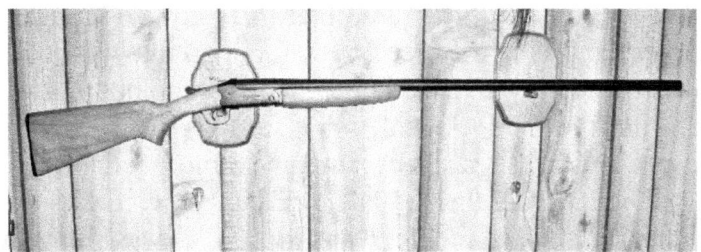

Weapons of Mass Destruction?

Gunpowder was invented by the Chinese many centuries ago, probably not too many centuries after Christ walked the earth. The gun, however, was not invented until many centuries after gunpowder. Of course, it was not called gunpowder until after the gun came along.

The first guns were cannons, and most believe they came into use just before the 1300s. These first crude weapons were made from logs with bands of iron wrapped around them to give them more strength. They fired stones and were not very effective.

Later, someone had the idea of making one out of iron and firing an iron ball. Now the first real gun was made, very simple, but effective. Over the years, the cannons became bigger and more powerful. They also became a little more accurate.

Once the cannon became popular, someone had the idea of making one very small, one that could be held in the hand and fired. It was known as the "hand cannon." This then led to one that had a wooden stock that could be placed on the shoulder and fired, therefore becoming even more accurate.

By the 1500s, firearms were common and were used in war. They were still crude by today's standards, but they worked. The most difficult problem was how to set off the charge that was in the breech. I will not go into all the inventions that were used to make the gun go boom, but by the 1700s the flintlock came into use. This was a great step forward and the firearms became much more reliable.

Then, during the 1840s the percussion cap was invented. This was another leap forward, as was rifling in the barrels. Before rifling, the barrels were smooth and accuracy was not very good.

The next step was the self-contained cartridge, which became popular beginning in the 1860s. After this, the cartridges changed from rimfire to centerfire. By this time, repeating guns were also gaining ground, the 1873 Winchester being one of the first popular guns.

Not long after this, the choke was invented for shotguns, giving the hunter more range in which to bring down his quarry. Soon after this, smokeless powder was introduced and we had what is today the modern cartridge.

All these modern inventions came soon after the Civil War in America. This was also the time that the greatest destruction of wildlife began. In the 1870s, hide hunters killed millions of bison until there were none roaming wild in the continental United States. There were just four bison left in Yellowstone National Park. Then two men sneaked in and shot two of them. Therefore, there were only two wild ones left, out of an estimated 60 million that once roamed America. Some farsighted Texas ranchers had captured around 500 and these animals, which were later used as breeding stock to replenish the decimated herds.

The passenger pigeon's nesting sites were also decimated, not with guns, but with nets, burning sulfur and by cutting down the trees to get the squabs. Trainloads of the young pigeons were shipped to restaurants in the east and sold for one and two cents apiece. How much is one worth today? No amount of money could buy one now because there are no more.

Other birds, such as ducks, geese, swans, shorebirds, egrets and others were also killed by the millions for their meat or feathers. The once abundant flocks were often reduced to a few thousand, a few hundred and in some cases, a few individuals.

The Eskimo curlew is probably extinct and other related shorebirds became uncommon or rare. The whooping crane was never very common and their population got down to about 15 individuals. This was in the early 1940s. When I was in the eighth-grade of school, in 1965, I remember our teacher saying that there were only 38 whooping cranes on earth. I also remember that I felt very sad that they were so few. They are the tallest bird in North America and one of the most magnificent. I have wanted to see one since I first heard of them. The photo on the next page I took in Indiana. It was my first sighting of a whooping crane. I had been waiting for over fifty years to see one. Even today, they are still very rare, but there is hope as their numbers continue to slowly climb.

It would take an entire book just to write about all the species that man has destroyed. The thylacine, Tasmanian wolf or Tasmanian tiger as some call it is gone because they were killed as pests. They were the largest marsupial predator on earth.

The title of this chapter is "Weapons of Mass Destruction." It is not guns that are the weapons of mass destruction, it is we humans. Many of the creatures on earth and their habitat, have been destroyed by not by guns, but by fire, bulldozers, nets, draining of swamps and other human activity. Even without guns, many animals would become rare or extinct. A gun is a tool, the same as any other. It can be used for good or evil. The greatest destruction is yet to come, and it will not come from guns, but will come from the results of human shortsightedness and their greed and selfishness.

It is easy to see that it is wrong to kill and destroy a species from off the face of the earth. But what about killing animals when their population is not threatened or for food?

Chapter 5

Dodo bird. Drawing by the author.

The Tide Turns

A couple of thousand years ago, there were still not many humans on earth. Wilderness was everywhere and so were plenty of animals. Slowly civilization began to grow and more and more land was developed. Then about a thousand years ago, things picked up and changes began to be a little more rapid. Many of the islands in the Pacific Ocean were settled, such as Hawaii. The birds and animals that lived there had little habitat because of being on an island. Most also had no fear of humans as they had never seen them. Man also brought pigs, dogs, and other animals with him when he settled new islands and lands.

On Hawaii, there was once a huge eagle, but it has been gone for so long that only a few bones have been found in some caves. Other birds have become extinct only recently, and a few were only discovered in the last few years and were nearly gone even before they were known to exist.

About the same time (a thousand years ago), the Polynesians arrived in New Zealand where the giant moa lived. It took about seven hundred years for the moa and its relatives to die out.

A cousin of the giant moa, and the largest bird to live in modern times was the elephant bird of Madagascar. It was up to ten feet tall and weighed about 1,000 pounds. It was plentiful until people first arrived there about 2,000 years ago, but before the year AD 1,000, they were gone.

The famous turkey-sized dodo bird of the island of Mauritius was in the pigeon family. It could not fly, even if it would have had fear of the newcomers to its home. The hogs and monkeys that were brought to the island in the 1500s destroyed their eggs, young and even adults. Sailors also killed many for food when they visited the island, and by 1680, the dodos were already extinct.

As mentioned earlier, North America was teaming with wildlife when the Native Americans were here. Shortly after the settlers came, they began to clear the land, build houses, towns and cities. Then roads and railroads where built to connect them. Dams were erected soon afterwards so boats could travel the waterways.

There were no game laws and birds and animals could be killed at any time of the year. It did not matter if they had young, were on the nest or if they were already rare.

The largest siren in the world was the Steller's sea cow. It was a giant manatee that lived in the cold Bering

Sea. It was not discovered until 1741, but by 1768, they were already extinct.

This was not the only rare animal that quickly disappeared from North America. Most have never even heard of the sea mink. This relative of the sea otter and the common mink, lived along the eastern seaboard. Only a few skins remain of this not very common animal. Likewise, the Labrador duck died out quickly because of its scarcity and pressure from humans. No one knows for sure why this very attractive duck was gone by 1878 but it was. Never common, its nesting grounds may have had human activity such as egg gathering or some other factor that lead to its demise.

The great auk, which was a flightless bird that took the place of the penguin in the northern hemisphere, was slaughtered by the tens of thousands, and was wiped out by the 1840s.

There also have been many subspecies of birds and animals that have disappeared from America. The plains grizzly, the Badlands big horn sheep and many others.

In the following chapters, I have several articles that I wrote long ago about the different birds and animals we have lost. After these chapters, I will discuss what is going on today and come back to the question of why this book was written. Is it wrong to kill animals?

Chapter 6

What We Have Lost

When America was first discovered by white man, the North American continent teamed with wildlife. Great herds of *Bison* or *Buffalo,* as most knew them, stretched from the Rockies in the west to the Atlantic coast. Their trails crisscrossed the west from Texas through the Great Plains into Canada and all across the Midwest. One trail in Indiana went from east to west just north of where the Interstate 64 highway would later be built.

Mountain Lions, along with *Black Bears* and *Elk* roamed our state, as did the *Gray Wolf. Red Wolves* were also in the southern part of Indiana. In the extreme southwestern tip of the state was the *Spotted Skunk*. In the north, was the *Lynx* and the largest member of the weasel family, the *Wolverine*. His cousin the *Fisher* and its prey the *Porcupine* inhabited the evergreen forest.

Whitetail Deer were everywhere and were an important food source for the Native Americans who lived here. Then there were birds of all kinds. The largest that roamed Indiana's hills was the *Eastern Wild Turkey*. Colorful parrots called the *Carolina Parakeet* were all over the state. In the southern part of the state, the magnificent *Ivory-billed Woodpecker* made its home. The skies were also filled with a bird that was so numerous that they blotted out the sun for days as they passed by—the *Passenger Pigeon*. The great *Bald Eagle* soared in our skies, and the swiftest of all birds on earth, the *Peregrine Falcon*, hunted its prey. *Sandhill Cranes* nested in the north, as did the *Whooping Crane* and the *Trumpeter Swan*. The *Raven's* call could also be heard as well as the honking of the giant race of *Canada Goose*.

Streams were not empty either. *Beavers* were plentiful, as were *River Otters*. On our prairies, *Prairie Chickens* did their courting dance and beside them, just north of where Terre Haute would later be, were a few *Pronghorn Antelope*.

Then in less than 157 years from the time Indiana became a state, and in most cases, less than 50 years, every bird and animal I have mentioned was gone. Some like the Carolina parakeet and passenger pigeon would be lost to the world forever. And not only were they lost, but others. There were some American birds and animals that almost no one even remembers. One was the sea mink that lived along the North Atlantic coast. Another was the *Heath Hen*, a type of prairie chicken that lived in the east. The beautiful *Labrador Duck* also lived along the East Coast, but disappeared by 1875. Out in the North Atlantic the *Great Auk* had already been slaughtered to extinction by the 1840s. A tame flightless bird similar to a penguin about two feet tall that nested on cold desolate islands was easy prey for men in ships. On the other side of the continent, in the North

Pacific near Alaska, once swam a giant relative of the Florida manatee, the *Steller's Sea Cow*. It, too, had been slaughtered and wiped from the face of the earth by the late 1700s. It also was a victim of man's greed. Just off our cost in Bermuda, a little petrel called a *Cahow* was slaughtered to extinction because of a famine that hit the island in the 1600s. At least it was thought to be extinct. Then after nearly 300 years, its call was once again heard, and a handful of individuals were found nesting on a tiny island close by.

One of our most recent birds to be lost has been the Bachman's warbler from our southern states. The *Ivory-billed Woodpecker* like the *Cahow* was thought to have been extinct until one was spotted in Louisiana after having not been seen for 60 years. No new reports have confirmed that they are still alive, however.

Many birds and animals almost went the same way. The *Bald Eagle, Peregrine Falcon, Trumpeter Swan, California Condor*, the tiny *Ross' Goose* and the *Aleutian Goose*, the *Whooping Crane* and the *Eskimo Curlew* along with many of its cousins of the sandpiper family. Even the *Wood Duck* became rare. Some of the animals that were almost lost were the *Bison, Musk Ox, Red Wolf, Black-footed Ferret, Sea Otter, Elephant Seal* and the American *Crocodile*. The list goes on and on with smaller animals, fish, amphibians, and even insects.

In Indiana, our last *Black Bear* was seen in 1850, the last *Cougar* in 1851. The *Gray Wolf* disappeared in 1908, the last *Red Wolf* in 1832. The last *Bison* and *Elk* faded from our state in 1830. The *Spotted Skunk* was gone by 1920. The *Beaver* was completely trapped out by 1845, and the last of the *Eastern Turkeys* were shot by 1904. The last native *Whitetail Deer* was killed in Knox County in 1893. The *last River Otter* was seen in Posey County at Hovey Lake in 1942 and the last *Prairie Chicken* disappeared from Indiana in 1972.

Others like the *Bobcat* and *Badger* are rare. The *Alligator Snapping Turtle* (the largest fresh water turtle in the world) and the *Swamp Rabbit*, both of which inhabit the southwestern tip of the state, are also rare. The *Swamp Rabbit*, which lives in only a few counties along the Ohio and Wabash Rivers, has nearly disappeared because of habitat destruction.

I could go on with the list of smaller animals; fish and reptiles that are gone or endangered like the largest salamander in North America, the *Hellbender*, which lives in only a few of the rivers in the southern tip of Indiana.

Some birds and animals have been brought back to Indiana like; the *Deer, Turkey, Beaver, Bald Eagle, Peregrine Falcon*, and most recently the *Otter*. The *Bobcat* and *Badger* have begun to increase and some birds have begun nesting here again, the *Sandhill Crane* is one, but others will never again inhabit our state because their habitat is gone and cannot be restored.

Not only species, but also many races of birds and animals in North America are gone forever. The *Eastern Elk*, the *Plains Grizzly*, the *Badlands Bighorn Sheep* and the *Dusky Seaside Sparrow* are a few that are now only history.

These are just the animals in North America; worldwide wildlife has disappeared and is now disappearing at an even faster rate. Tasmania lost its largest marsupial predator the *Tasmanian Wolf* or *Tasmanian Tiger* as some call it. The most famous and one of the first creatures to disappear because of man was the flightless *Dodo* bird. Not long afterwards, the largest of all birds, the *Giant Moa* and the *Elephant Bird* were added to the list.

What will happen if things continue as they are? As the fabric of our planet is torn away piece by piece, the land, air and water polluted and destroyed along with its creatures, we too will go the way of the dodo and others like it. This planet can only take so much destruction and it too will get rid of the *"disease"* that is causing its suffering. We are like a modern-day Noah, able to save what is here if we choose to or stand by and watch our world die all around us. If our past is any indication of our future, only *God Almighty* will be able to save our world and us.

An update: Since I first wrote this. The ruffed grouse is nearly gone now from Indiana, and probably soon will be. They were getting more common after the 1930s when many Hoosier farms became abandoned during the Great Depression. Now, because of habitat loss over the last thirty years, they are almost gone. It seems a shame that Indiana sportsmen spends millions of dollars for licenses, habitat stamps and taxes to help game management; then, the ones in authority, the ones that are supposed to guard our birds and animals, lets a marvelous bird such as the ruffed grouse slip into oblivion.

Chapter 7

Indiana Black Bears

(Mounted bear above is a Kentucky black bear at Kingdom Come State Park)

Back in 1995, I wrote several articles in my newspaper columns about the disappearance of many of our native birds and animals. One was about the cougar and the other was about black bears. I said in both, that if things continue as they have, it would only be a matter of time until the cougar and black bear could return to Indiana. The cougar disappeared in 1851, and it indeed found its way back just a few years ago. It is not yet breeding, but give it time. The black bear has not yet returned, but just across the Ohio River, they have been seen in central and north central Kentucky, near Owensboro. The only thing stopping them from reaching Indiana is a short swim across the river.

This past Labor Day (2013), my wife Lilly and I visited some of her relatives in Eastern Kentucky, in Perry County. This area is in the middle of the range of Kentucky's elk herd and where black bears first showed up many years ago. The bear is now very common there and even a nuisance. We went there last year also, but I was not lucky enough to see a bear. We even went driving around at night hoping to see one, but didn't even get a glimpse. We did find out later, that only a half mile from the house where we were staying, a bear had raided a neighbor's garbage can that very night.

Lilly's cousin on the mountainside, just above where we were, often has black bears tearing up her bird feeders and stealing bags of dog food from the back of their pick-up truck. Lilly's aunt that lives across the road from her cousin, has had bears come into the carport and attempt to open an old, up-right freezer where dog food is stored. Muddy paw prints were left behind along with dents in the freezer to show the bear's frustration at not being able to get to the food. This past year, after storing the dog food elsewhere, the bears knocked over the freezer to try to open it with the hope there was still something inside for them to eat. The bears have also torn down her humming bird feeders on the front porch. She even saw one looking in her living room window early one morning.

While visiting Cumberland, KY, Lilly and I went to Kingdom Come State Park, which is only a few miles from where we were staying. They have bear crossing signs posted and a gift shop near a lake. Inside the gift shop, they have a black bear on display that was recently mounted. The bear was hit by a vehicle while trying to cross a major highway just a few miles away.

I do not know if black bears will show up in Indiana in my lifetime, but if there is still some habitat left and they continue to increase in Kentucky, it is only a matter of time before there will once again be Indiana black bears.

An update: According to a comment on the Internet, a black bear was sighted in the northwestern part of Indiana on April 20, 2012, at 1:05 pm on I-65 at the 220-mile marker. The gentleman, Bob Haskin, who saw it, said that he got a good look at the bear as it ran across an open area. He also said that he and several cars pulled over to see the bear. In addition, again this year (2015), another credible sighting of a black bear has been reported in northern Indiana. Evidently, they have wondered in from Michigan.

Ya, right!

Black bears could return to Indiana

KENNY BARNES
OUTDOORS COLUMNIST

Martin Luther Vaasda was born near Newburgh Dec. 4, 1812. According to a May 25, 1909 *Evansville Courier* article, he, as a young man, killed a bear within a hundred yards of his home in Warrick County. This must have been in the mid to late 1830s, for by 1850 black bears were gone from Indiana.

In the early settlement of our state, bears were very plentiful and were a valuable food source to the pioneers. Not only was their flesh eaten, but their skins made warm covering on cold nights (it's said that, as a child, Abraham Lincoln used a bear skin for this purpose). The fat was also used by being made into bear grease.

But besides being valuable, bears were often destructive to livestock. Back in those days, more people let their hogs run free in the forest to fend for themselves on acorns or whatever they could find. Bears would often make a quick and easy meal of the pigs.

This couldn't make the settlers happy and the bear was looked numbers. It worked, and their population began to rise. Soon bears were being seen in Missouri.

With protection, bear populations in other states also started to rebound. In the last several years, bears have moved into Kentucky from West Virginia, Virginia and Tennessee. They were thought to be gone from the state by 1900, but occasional reports of sightings in remote parts of the Cumberland Plateau continued through the 1970s.

Then documented sightings in the early '80s increased until today. Reliable reports are now being come to backyard bird feeding stations; they have even been known to sleep the winter months under the floor of an occupied home.

One man in Ohio was hunting groundhogs when a bear came out of the woods near him. After killing the bear, he claimed self-defense, but was cited on charges of taking a bear out of season.

I received information that two bears were released in the Shawnee Nation Forest in Illinois; one was soon shot and the other hit by a car. I also have reliable information that a few bears exist, or occasionally wander into the southern part of Illinois from Missouri.

So, what are the prospects for bears one day returning to Indiana? Indiana is one of the few states that do not have any bears. Only South Dakota, Delaware, Rhode Island, Iowa and Illinois are not supposed to have bears. This information comes from an article written in 1981; it also mentioned Ohio as not having any, but this, of course, has changed.

It also seems logical that, if things continue as they are, in several a tea kettle. If it was a bear, I don't know why, or how, it got there. But I do remember the tracks very well—they had three inch claw marks protruding from them.

Bears often travel waterways and have been known to travel a hundred miles or so after returning to an area where they had been captured and released.

Black bears are large animals. One killed in Wisconsin weighed over 800 pounds. The world record is over 900 pounds for one in Arizona. Since they are large, and have teeth and claws, bears can be dangerous and there are many cases of black bears killing humans.

Usually, however, they're shy and try to stay away from people, and are not often seen, even in areas where they are common. But once they get over their shyness, bears can become a nuisance.

One in Ohio got in the habit of raiding a dumpster that contained the remains of ice cream containers and cake frosting. After being trapped, tagged and transported to a

This was someone's joke where I worked. Evidently, they thought that a bear could never return to Indiana. I also predicted the cougar would return. There have been at least two confirmed reports of cougars in Indiana since 2011.

Chapter 8

The Wanderer of Little Pigeon Creek

Passing an old tarpaper covered one-room shack, I walked down a slightly sloping hill. Going a few more steps, I came to a huge sycamore tree that sat on the muddy bank of a stream that was a stone's toss across. The sky was bright blue that mid-October day what little I could see of it, for the tall golden and crimson overhanging maple trees formed a tunnel over the creek making it rather dark. Large patches of sunshine, however, did manage to reach the forest floor here and there.

As I moved passed the sycamore, I was suddenly startled as a mass of green, red and yellow birds that were chattering and screaming came rushing from a large hole in the hollow tree just over my head. They were Carolina parakeets and seemed angry that I had disturbed them. The tree evidently was their roosting place. Coming out of the tree, I could see their long tapering tails, pointed wings and their near comical face. The noisy flock of 13 birds flew close together up stream through the tunnel of trees. I stood watching as their brilliant green plumage glistened as they passed through the patches of sunlight that filtered through the trees. I watched until they were out of sight and to where I couldn't hear their vociferous chattering any longer.

"Finally, peace and quiet," I thought, taking my seven-foot willow pole and reaching into the can to retrieve one of the red earthworms. Baiting my hook, I walked to the edge of the water and tossed in the line. After anchoring the end of the pole in the soft mud I sat back to relax and enjoy the afternoon.

I loved coming here to fish. I was born on its' muddy banks in a back room of my grandmother's old three-room house, which sat overlooking the creek.

Sitting there, I heard a loud splash up stream and looked to see a large wave rippling across the water where a big fish had come to the surface. The water was cooler now and fish often seemed to enjoy coming to the surface and showing off.

Turning my attention back to my line, I glanced at the cork bobber, wondering if the huge fish may be coming down stream towards me and my baited hook.

As I thought about how good a platter of golden-brown fish would taste, I heard the unmistakable sound of whirling wings of wood ducks as they were lifting from the water.

Looking down stream, I heard the females uttering their high-pitched call as I saw a flock of perhaps thirty ducks lift into the air. Speeding down the creek, they flew up and over the tops of the trees and were gone. The families that had hatched this year were now gathering, getting ready for their long migration south. "They must have been swimming upstream and seen me." I thought.

Suddenly I saw my cork move, and then it began bobbing up and down as it traveled across the surface of the water. Pulling the pole from the muddy bank, I held it on the ready to set the hook. The cork suddenly disappeared out of sight in the murky water and I yanked on the line.

A large bluegill came up from the depths of the creek and I took hold of the line with my left hand. Carrying the pole and fish to the top of the bank, I removed the hook and picked up a stringer that I had already prepared. After slipping the stick at one end of the stringer through the fish's mouth and gill, I returned it to the water, re-baited my hook, and tossed out the line again.

Sitting there waiting for the next fish to bite, I heard something in the distance. "Was that thunder?" I thought. "It sounds like it, yet it doesn't. It sounded more like a roar."

Standing on the bank listing, it began getting dark. "It must be a storm coming because it's only about 3 o'clock and it won't be getting dark for three or more hours".

The sound then began getting closer and the roar louder. "That's not thunder, but what in the world is it?"

Suddenly the roar became deafening and the sky overhead through the trees looked as if a great shadow was sweeping over it. Looking at the trees, I saw them begin to move. There was no breeze before, but now the wind was picking up and the treetops started moving. I could feel the air moving all around me. "It must be a storm," I thought, "but it can't be." Then a feeling of awe swept over me as the wind picked up with gale force and tears came into my eyes. The trees were now swaying and moving along with everything around me from the great wind. The sky was now so black that I could not see any blue in it.

As the wind moved all around me, it began to rain, but the rain was white! "That's not rain," I thought as it fell on every bush and tree and the ground around me. "It is bird droppings!" I had heard tell of what I was witnessing, but I could not even fathom the awesomeness of the spectacle that was before me.

I could not hear anything but the roaring of millions of wings. I could see the wind moving everything, but the thunderous sound above me was too loud to hear anything else.

Looking to my left, I happen to notice that two men were standing nearby. It was old man Finley and his son Uly from the one room shack. Finley had a double-barreled twelve-gauge shotgun and his son had a single-shot of the same gauge. Their pockets were bulging with shells as they raised their guns to fire.

Everything seemed unreal. I saw the blast of the guns and I could see the smoke bellowing from the barrels, but I could not hear them go off, the roaring above me was just too great.

As they continued to fire, it began raining down birds all around me. Some fell motionless and others fell into the creek and began drifting downstream. Some were only wounded and began trying to get up and flutter back into the air to join their comrades passing overhead.

Thousands and then tens of thousands of birds began landing in the trees all along the creek. So many birds filled the limbs of the great trees that even the giant oaks could not take the strain of their weight and began to brake and the limbs and birds came crashing to the ground killing many. Again, I could see the limbs falling but could not hear what I was witnessing.

Looking back at the men, they had stopped shooting, their pockets empty now of the shells but still staring; mesmerized it seems at the great sight they were seeing.

A minute or two later, they broke their gaze into the sky and began picking up some of the birds. With both hands full, they tucked their shotguns under their arm and walked up the hill and disappeared.

All around me were still hundreds of dead and wounded birds. Feathers littered the ground, bushes and trees. Blood was sprinkled here and there amongst the white covered forest floor. Birds, feathers and droppings clogged the creek and gently floated down stream. I then looked to see painted-shell turtles gathering at the surface to dine on the bodies of the unfortunate victims.

Standing there, I looked down to see one of the birds on the ground beside me. Reaching down, I picked up its warm limp body. It was a little larger than a mourning dove. It had a long tapering tail like the dove, but its back was bluish gray and its breast pink. It was a male and very handsome. A female lay on the ground just to my left; she was very plain colored, just gray, with some white on her belly and tail. "They must have come from Michigan or Wisconsin," I thought. "That's where their enormous nesting colonies are; their last great stronghold. I've heard that perhaps two billion nest there. I also heard that once there were two or three times as many as there are now. The ones in the east are now nearly gone. Someone told me, too, that the Narragansett Indians called him *Wuskowhan*, which means the wanderer."

I stood in amazement at the sight and sound all around me. It all seemed like a dream and it was, for I was born April 4, 1951, on the banks of Little Pigeon Creek at the southern tip of Indiana. This is several miles downstream from Gentryville, where Abraham Lincoln grew up and near the Ohio River. Now, however, the creek sits empty of its namesake because I was born about one hundred years too late to have seen what I just described. The last passenger pigeon, named Martha, died September 1, 1914 at the Cincinnati Zoo, thus finally and forever ending her species.

As a child, I often wondered why the creek was named so because I never saw a pigeon anywhere near it. Now its muddy banks will never again see the sky darkened with the great migrating flocks that once passed by. Neither I nor my children or grandchildren or will anyone else ever again see one of the greatest spectacles of the world: the wanderer of Little Pigeon Creek.

Chapter 9

A Living Storm

*(This was my first story about the passenger pigeon. It is similar, but different from **The Wanderer of Little Pigeon Creek** and I wanted to include it.)*

On April 4, 1951, I was born at my grandmother's house along Little Pigeon Creek in Warrick County, Indiana.

Growing up on the creek in Southern Indiana was good for a little boy. There were newly hatched wood ducks in the spring and baby turtles and frogs to catch. Even a great horned owl nested in a huge sycamore tree on the bank of the creek where my dad and I used to fish. However, as a small child, I often wondered why everyone called it Pigeon Creek; for I never saw pigeons anywhere near it.

Only after I was older, did I learn why it was named as it was, and why there were no pigeons there. When I did learn of the reason it was so named, I was saddened, because at one time, its muddy banks witnessed the greatest numbers of any bird or animal species on earth.

Early in the 1800s, passenger pigeons swarmed over the creek in numbers that cannot even be imagined today. An early naturalist, Alexander Wilson, while traveling between Franklin, Kentucky and the Indiana territory in 1810, saw a flight of passenger pigeons, which he estimated at over 2 billion. Three years later, John James Audubon saw a flight between Louisville and Henderson, Kentucky, which he numbered well over 1 billion.

The passenger pigeon was a beautiful bird, resembling the mourning dove, but being slightly larger. The male had a blue back with a pink breast and a long tapering tail. The female was rather drab like its cousin, the dove.

There were many differences, however. The mourning dove lays two eggs and nests several times a season. The passenger pigeon only laid one egg, and it was believed to have raised just one offspring each year, much like the band-tailed pigeon of our western states. Also like the band-tail, it nested in large flocks. Some of these nesting areas were so large as to stagger the imagination of those who observed them. A nesting colony in Wisconsin was the largest ever found; its size was seventy-five miles long by ten to fifteen miles wide. This nesting area was some seven hundred and fifty square miles, and each tree had dozens of nests in it.

Few however, ever witnessed these great nesting sites, but in the fall when they began their migration south, it was a different story. The Narragansett Indians called him Wuskowhan, the wanderer, and part of their scientific name means, the one that migrates.

Like a storm cloud of life, they moved over the land, going south in autumn and north in spring. Traveling at thirty to forty miles an hour, it would often take them days to pass by. The flights would be two miles wide and hundreds of miles long, and so dense that the sun would be darkened as if by a solar eclipse.

When coming to roost, it was said that their wings produced gale force winds and a deafening roar. So loud would be the noise of their beating wings, that if a man fired a shotgun from only a few feet away, it could not be heard.

Large trees where the birds landed to roost in, could often not hold the great weight of their numbers and would come crashing down, killing many of them. Afterwards, when the birds left their roosting area, it appeared as if a tornado had devastated the trees. The forest floor would be white, looking like snow, where two or three inches of their droppings had fallen.

Once they ranged over the entire eastern half of the United States. To the early settlers, they were sometimes a blessing, and at other times, a curse. Swarming into their crops, they would destroy the vital grain. If, however, they arrived after the crops were in, or if the crops had failed, they were an important food supply.

So, what happened to them? How could a creature with numbers so great completely disappear in such a short time?

The Indians had used them as food for centuries. In the East, they often brought young pigeons to the settlements to trade to the pilgrims. However, as the land was cleared and many of their food sources: acorns, beechnuts, and other foods disappeared along with the great forest that they nested in; their numbers began to diminish. This, along with the commercial destruction of their nesting areas was the greatest cause for their decline. For if they had only been shot during their migration, there would be no way that their numbers could have suffered so much, so quickly. One shot could usually bring down only a dozen or so birds, and back in the early 1800s, it was too expensive for the average person to "waste" shells on such small game.

It was the wholesale destruction of their nesting and roosting sights that quickly destroyed them. Their numbers had noticeably decreased in the East by the middle 1800s, and by the 1870s the slaughter began in earnest. In 1875, a wealthy farmer from Ohio, along with hundreds of men, invaded a nesting colony in Newaygo County, Michigan. Using nets, which could catch up to 3,000 or more pigeons at a time, and cutting down the trees to obtain squabs, they began the task. The estimated take from this nesting colony was between 40 and 50 *tons* of birds, to be sold to restaurants for one and two cents apiece!

In 1878, another nesting site was found. It was the *last* great nesting colony of passenger pigeons on earth. Within a few weeks, 2,500 men with nets took an unbelievable number of pigeons, which was over one billion one hundred million! A smaller nesting area yielded one million birds in 1881.

By this time, the pigeons were doomed, even though the men with the nets had gone home and there were still thousands left. The few that did remain were still being persecuted, and the last shipment of a handful of birds was received from Arkansas in 1893. Wisconsin saw its last passenger pigeon in 1899, and the last one to fall by man's destruction was killed by a boy in Ohio in March of 1900. After this, none were reported killed. A flock of 200 was seen in Michigan in 1903, and scattered reports continued two or three years later, but by this time there was only one passenger pigeon known to exist on earth. In the Cincinnati, Zoological Garden lived Martha, the last of her kind. Then on September 1, 1914, at 1 o'clock p.m. she died, thus finally and forever ending her species.

So why did the passenger pigeon disappear? Because of greed, and disregard of our responsibility to take care of the earth. If governmental authorities would have passed laws to protect their nesting sites, they still could be with us today.

Did anyone learn anything from the loss of one of God's creatures? Laws were passed a long time later to protect some birds and animals, but only after many were already gone.

In our world today, birds and animals continue to become extinct, and the number one cause is habitat destruction. It seems a shame, and is, that we no longer have the passenger pigeon. Attempts to collect them for breeding came too late. Even if they could have been bred in captivity, it is doubtful they could have existed in the wild. It seems they needed large areas to breed in, and an uninterrupted supply of food on their migration route. With much of the forest destroyed, there were gaps on their journeys and many of their ancestral nesting sites were gone. Only with large areas set aside for them to nest in could they have survived. They also needed large numbers of themselves because of their low reproduction rate.

The band-tailed pigeon nearly had the same fate, but was protected in time. It has since adapted somewhat to man, and is even seen at backyard feeding stations. I would have hoped the passenger pigeon could have adapted too, but we shall never know.

So now, the place I was born sits empty of its namesake. Its muddy banks will never again see the sky darkened with the great flocks that once passed by. I, nor will anyone else ever again see the wanderer of Little Pigeon Creek.

Note: Much of the information about the passenger pigeon in these last two stories, are from a book by Peter Matthiessen. His book was published in 1959.

Chapter 10

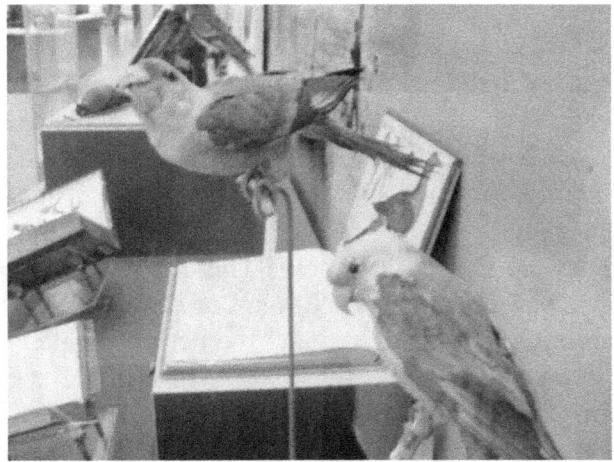

Forever Lost:

The Carolina Parakeet

In the last century and a half, we have lost a host of indigenous birds and animals from North America. A few we have managed to bring back, like the whitetail deer, the turkey and the beaver. Others, however, have been gone for so long that many people do not even know they once lived here and will never be brought back, because they are extinct. The Labrador duck, sea mink, passenger pigeon and Carolina parakeet are some that are gone forever.

The Carolina parakeet was a beautiful bird that was once common in the eastern half of the United States. A few thick-billed parrots once lived just north of the Mexican border, but disappeared many years ago. An effort was made to reintroduce them to Arizona, but failed. Other than this, the Carolina parakeet was the only parrot species to live and nest in the United States.

When our country was first being settled, the Carolina parakeet was very common. This small green parrot, with a yellow and orange head, traveled in noisy flocks and was often seen along the Ohio River where I grew up. They were fond of seeds of the cocklebur weed, and Audubon's famous painting of them, shows several of the parrots in such a bush.

Why aren't they here now? There are several reasons.

Back in the early days of our country, there were no laws protecting birds or animals. If a person wanted to kill or capture an animal to eat, sell, or just for the sake of killing it, there was nothing to stop them.

One of the reasons they quickly disappeared was because they were very destructive to orchards. Always on the move to find food, they would flock to an orchard and proceed to tear apart the fruit. This habit made them very unpopular with the early settlers who depended on the food they raised to sustain them throughout the year.

A peculiar behavior, however, made them even more susceptible to extinction. While feeding in a tree, all it would take was for one to be shot, and this usually assured the destruction of the entire flock. If the birds would have been frightened and flown away, they may have survived, but they did not. When one of their companions fell, they would fly around overhead squawking and lighting again and again until all were killed. Many parakeets were also killed this way to obtain feathers for women's hats.

Not only were they killed for being destructive to fruit trees and for their beautiful feathers, but many were also captured and sold as pets.

Since the birds were very intelligent and would become tame in only a few days, they were in high demand.

Another behavior of theirs made it very easy to capture them. They roosted in hollow trees, which was one of their downfalls. For a person with a gunnysack could hold the sack over the entrance, while someone else struck the tree with a stick. The frightened birds would then rush out of the tree into the sack, and the entire flock would be captured.

By the middle of the 1800s, the parakeet's numbers were beginning to dwindle, and they had disappeared from most of their former range. Once they lived from the East Coast, through the Midwest as far west as Kansas and eastern Texas, and south to Florida. By 1900, only a handful held out in the most remote parts of Florida. It was in this state that the last tiny flock of Carolina parakeets was seen a few years later.

The last Carolina parakeet died in captivity in 1918, at the Cincinnati Zoo according to most authorities. I have also read that it was 1914 or 1920. There was even a claim that a small flock was "rediscovered" in 1930, but all that doesn't really matter, because now this earth is empty of their presence.

In the early 1800s, naturalist Alexander Wilson and Audubon saw them in great numbers along rivers and streams in Kentucky and Southern Indiana where I grew up. Wilson once described how beautiful they were with the sun shining on their brilliant green plumage as a huge flock lifted from the Ohio River and landed in nearby trees.

I have sometimes sat at my window, in the winter, watching mourning doves flocking to my feeder, alighting in the leafless maple tree above it. I have tried to imagine how it would be if we still had the Carolina parakeet. I could easily picture them in my mind flying across the yard in a small flock and lighting in the tree. Here they would sit, looking down at the tray of sunflower seeds. They would be chattering amongst themselves and pulling themselves up to the next branch with their strong bill as all parrots do today. They would also be "talking" with one another about what they had discovered. I could see their long tapering tails, which were much like the doves, and their brilliant green

43

feathers glistening in the early morning sunshine. Being only about 14 inches long, there would be room for several to be sitting on the feeder while the others were chattering above them in the tree.

If they would have survived to more recent times, with all the modern methods of captive breeding, artificial incubation, and radio transmitters for tracking their movements, they may have been saved. In fact, because of birdhouse erections, backyard-feeding stations, and a different attitude toward wildlife today, they may have made a strong comeback as the wood duck did. They may have even become too numerous and control measures would have had to be taken to protect fruit crops. There probably would be thousands of small flocks throughout the eastern United States. It could have been possible for them to even extend their range as some birds have done due to feeding stations.

This, however, did not happen, and now I can only see them in my mind. I will never see them flocking to a large hollow sycamore tree at dusk along Little Pigeon Creek where I grew up, as they did long ago. I will never see a young one with its all green plumage leaving an old woodpecker hole for its first flight. Not only will I not see them, but also my children will not, nor my children's children. Nor will anyone else.

The woods are a little emptier now, and will never again hear the joyful chattering of our only native North American parrot. For we have lost forever one of God's creations. We have forever lost the Carolina parakeet.

Chapter 11

The Greatest of Them all:
The Ivory-billed Woodpecker

(This was first published in my newspaper column in 1993)

He was the greatest of his kind in North America. When the colonists first arrived, vast forests covered the eastern half of our nation. And in this virgin timber, lived a giant woodpecker: the ivory-billed. Most plentiful in the South, where cypress trees grew, it haunted the dark forests from where Texas would later be, to Florida and the Carolinas. They ranged as far north as Illinois and Southern Indiana where I was born.

Northern Indians traveled south to trade for its bill, which was highly prized for ornamentation. Nevertheless, that was long ago. The last confirmed sighting of this great bird in the United States was in 1946, in northern Louisiana.

There are many kinds of woodpeckers in North America, but only one can even be compared to the ivory-billed. The slightly smaller pileated looks similar, but has more black, and the female pileated looks almost identical to the male. The ivory-billed on the other hand, has much more white on it, and the female is nearly all black. Both species have a large red crest, except for the female ivory-billed, which is black. The crow-size pileated's call is a series of high-pitched notes in rapid succession; the ivory-billed's is a single high-pitched one, sounding similar to the white-breasted nuthatch's call of "yank".

What makes the ivory-billed's story so sad, is that it didn't have to come to the verge of extinction. We had already lost the passenger pigeon, Carolina parakeet, Labrador duck, heath hen and sea mink. Others like the Eskimo curlew, whooping crane, trumpeter swan, and bison were also nearly gone. Conservationists tried to halt the destruction of the forest where the woodpeckers lived, but didn't succeed, and the last area where it was certain that they existed was destroyed.

At the time, most people in authority said the woodpecker was already gone and wouldn't do anything to help. There were people who knew they were not extinct and tried to get the government to try to save them, but were ignored.

The ivory-billed woodpecker needs very large tracts of forest to survive. Forest where they feed on insects and grubs under the bark of trees, trees that have been dead for a while. This, however, caused problems for politicians. It cost money to buy large areas of land, and it may offend some who want to cut down all the trees, and this would cost them a few votes. It is much easier to say the bird is extinct and cannot be helped.

But how much is an ivory-billed woodpecker worth? Some would argue that if they can't tolerate the changes that human activity cause, then they should die out. But who are we to push one of God's creations off the face of the earth.

Why can't we live with nature instead of destroying it; for if we destroy nature, we will inevitably destroy ourselves. What right do we have to take away something that can never be replaced; something our descendants will never get to enjoy?

I resent our forefathers for not preserving the passenger pigeon and the other creatures like it. I miss the Carolina parakeet and the Labrador duck. No one had the right to destroy them all.

What is an ivory-billed woodpecker worth? Can a price even be placed on the worth of a species? All the money, time and effort in the world cannot bring them back once they're gone.

Every creature on our planet is worth the time and money to save, if they're in trouble, and to save them while there is still hope. For some day, we too will have to answer to future generations. The questions will be, "Why didn't you save the birds and animals for us to see and enjoy? What right did you have to destroy the things that belonged to everyone?" Not only will we have to answer to future generations, we will have to answer to the Creator who designed and placed them on earth for us to have stewardship over.

Today there is but a tiny glimmer of hope for the ivory-billed. A few were recently discovered in eastern Cuba (an estimated dozen or so) living in a remote mountain forest, a forest that is being cut down. No one knows how long they can hold on, for this was several years ago, now. They are most certainly gone now.

As I write this, there are continued reports of the ivory-billed being sighted in some of our southern states. Nearly every year there are such reports. In most cases, it is probably the pileated woodpecker being seen. There are, however, knowledgeable people who bring in reports every once in a while. Therefore, there still may be a few clinging on to existence in the United States. The glimmer of hope, however, is dimming more each day as the land is cleared and the wild places are growing smaller and smaller.

We can only hope that if there are a few, they will struggle even harder to adapt and live near man, as has their cousin, the pileated. We can also hope that attention is given by everyone to the remaining wild areas that we have left, so they will be protected; thus helping, not only the ivory-billed, but all wildlife.

In our eastern forests, we can see the red-bellied woodpecker, little downy, his bigger cousin the hairy, the yellow-shafted flicker, and the red-headed. In winter, you can find the colorful yellow-bellied sapsucker. Also, in the South, lives a few of the endangered red-cockaded woodpeckers. In places where the woods are large enough, we can still find the impressive pileated. But unless a miracle takes place, you will never see the greatest woodpecker of them all: the ivory-billed.

Footnote: A miracle may have taken place. I wrote an earlier version of this article for my newspaper column in 1993. Recently, as you probably have heard, an Ivory-billed was seen in Louisiana. If they have survived all these years, then there may still be hope for the greatest woodpecker of them all.

Chapter 12

A white grey squirrel. Photo by the author.

Today

Today, thousands of different species of animals are being killed or pushed out of their ever-shrinking habitat. The African elephant, pictured above, is being slaughtered for its ivory tusks. It, along with the Asian elephant, has smaller and smaller habitat in which to live, even if they were plentiful. Animals, like humans, must have food, shelter, and protection in order to flourish. You can protect them all you want, but if there is not any place for them to find food and raise their young, they will die out.

The human population has soared in the last century and continues to climb more and more each day. More land is being cleared. Jungles are being replaced by giant farms that grow only one crop. Deserts are spreading and becoming larger. Farmland is being destroyed and, in its place, subdivisions and shopping malls are being built. Land is being strip-mined and waterways changed. Swamps are being filled in and people are building right beside streams and rivers. Then when floods come, they wonder why their homes are swept away. Just as the people did two hundred years ago, they do not think very far into the future. You would think that we would have learned by now, but you would be wrong. What will the earth be like in a hundred or five hundred years if it continues as it is? The answer is that it will not exist with life on it, at least not much life. Isiah 5: 8 says, "Woe unto them that join house to house, that lay field to field, till there be no place, that they may be placed alone in the midst of the earth!"

Every time you watch a nature film, which I love, you see that the natural world is getting smaller and smaller. More and more animals are being pushed into extinction. Where will it end? It will not end, and that is the sad truth. How do I know this?

The Creator of the universe has said many centuries ago what will happen in our time. Just like the newspapers or telecasts of today, the headlines in the Holy Scriptures has already aired. They have already been printed and released.

What does it say you might ask? The Bible talks about the trade of ivory making people wealthy near the end of our civilization, Revelation 18:12.

It also speaks about people filling the "face of the earth with cities," Isiah 14:21. In addition, it speaks about "destroying those that destroy the earth", Revelation 11:18.

With this said, is it wrong to kill an animal? It all depends on what animals and why. In days gone by, people had to kill many kinds of animals to protect their livestock and even themselves. This is still true today, but not nearly as much. Most big predators are gone or not common in or

50

around big cities. This is rapidly changing, however, in some places. Because man has destroyed much of the habitat that animals need, the animals are sometimes wandering into places where humans live and causing problems. People have built homes right in wilderness areas; or at least what were once wilderness areas. Some animals have become accustomed to humans and do not have much fear of them any longer. They are protected and cannot be killed; therefore, they now see humans as no threat. This can be bad. The killing of people by "beasts of the earth" is also predicted in the Bible, and it is in Revelation 6:8. "Beasts" could also mean germs, viruses, other pestilences, or all of the above, which most likely it will be.

You must remember that animals have no conscience, they do not know right from wrong. If you are a threat to them or their young, they will not feel any guilt, sadness or remorse if they rip you apart and kill you. If they are hungry, you are no different to them than a deer or rabbit in their mind.

When America was first settled, the grey wolf was widespread and was very common throughout the United States. The coyote on the other hand was restricted to the west. After the red wolf and timber or grey wolf were killed and driven out of the eastern part of America, the coyote, being very opportunistic, began to expand its range. Today, they are very common and have even taken up residence in large cities. Here they have become accustomed to humans and have lost their fear to a great extent and sometimes have even attracted people. Most of the time they attack and kill dogs and cats, but more and more often they have begun to attack children and even adults. I even had a neighbor recently that had a coyote come into his field near his home and attack his beagle. He had to drive it off to make it stop trying to kill his dog.

The same has happened with cougars and bears. The cougar or mountain lion was totally gone from the eastern

United States except for a remnant population of the Florida panther. After they were protected, their population began to increase and they began to spread into areas that they had not been in for over a hundred and fifty years. The same goes for black bears.

Today, we are in a place that humans have never been in before. For countless centuries, we did not have the power to destroy many plants or animals from the earth. Now we have not only the power to destroy many animals, we have the power to destroy all life, including our own from the face of our world. This was also predicted in the Bible. In Matthew 24:22, the Lord said that if He did not intervene and end man's destruction of the earth and his fellow man, "no flesh would be saved alive."

Yes, man has painted himself into a corner. God knew this from the beginning, however. When He gave man free will, He knew what would happen. This is why He had *a plan* to save mankind from himself, and He had this plan even from the foundation of the world. If you wish to learn more, you need to read my book *Mysteries of the Bible.*

What does this have to do with the killing of animals? In our world today, there are times that we must kill an animal either to eat, save another animal, save a human life or to even save the species. The earth, as I said earlier, has never been in the place it is now. Things are not natural. I have a chapter from my book; *Do Pets go to Heaven,* which I will include in this book to show what I mean. It is called *The Balance of Nature* and our world today is out of balance.

Chapter 13

An American badger

The Balance of Nature

(Much of this chapter is an excerpt from my book "Do Pets go to Heaven?")

Most of us can remember during biology class or in science class, hearing about the balance of nature. If you watch very many nature shows on television, as I do, you will soon see predators killing and eating their prey. As I said earlier, in the natural world, every creature born must die. This is true of every bird, animal, reptile or fish and even us. If an animal is born, it must die. This is a fact of nature and of life. It is not pleasant, but it is true.

The world is made up of predators and prey animals. The predators kill and eat the prey animals to keep them from becoming over populated. When a prey species becomes plentiful, the predators will have more food, which enables them to raise more young. As the predators increase, the prey decreases, then it goes back the other way. The predators then do not have enough food to raise many young so the prey once again begins to increase because of fewer predators. This balancing of predator and prey keeps both populations in check. Why is this?

We must first go back to the beginning and see. Adam and Eve were the first humans on earth. Is this true? Many believe so, but the Bible does not say this. This will surprise most. It says that "Eve is the mother of all living." It does not say that she is the mother of all that have ever lived. I cannot go into all the details of this because it would take too long. I do have much more about this in my commentary in the book, *CHRIST: His Words, His Life*. I also go into greater detail about this, and several other topics, in another of my books called *Mysteries of the Bible*.

In the Garden of Eden, which God had planted, He said that the "green herbs" were for food, Genesis 1:30. This means we were originally meant to be vegetarians. After man sinned, God had to kill an animal to clothe them. Since that time, humans have killed animals and eaten meat.

I love friend chicken and hamburgers, as do most of us. There is nothing wrong with eating meat if you do not eat too much of it. Too much of anything can be harmful to you. However, in order to eat meat, an animal must die. This is just a fact. Someday this will change and be as it was meant to be in the Garden of Eden, but this is not true today. I will speak about this later.

As I said, some people do not eat meat and are vegetarians. There is nothing wrong in being a vegetarian and someday everyone on earth will be a vegetarian.

I am an outdoor writer and I write about hunting, fishing, birds, animals and conservation. President Teddy Roosevelt was a great conservationist, but he was also a hunter. He loved being in the outdoors where he liked to fish and hunt game. He saw that as long as animals had a place to live, had food and were protected so their population would stay high enough to reproduce themselves, there would always be plenty of animals. This president was responsible for establishing many of our national parks, including Yellowstone.

Killing of wild animals sometimes is a controversial topic. I understand the feelings that some have about killing an animal. There are two sides to the augment and I will give what I think is a balanced view and then say what God says about it.

As I said, every creature that is born must die, and this is an unpleasant fact. In the wild, millions of creatures a day die, from insects to giant whales. Predators kill many. Others are killed by accidents such as falling, drowning or being hit by cars on the highway. Many others die because of disease or starvation. There are countless ways that animals die.

Besides wild animals dying, there are hundreds of thousands of domestic animals dying each day because we kill them to eat. Chickens, turkeys, ducks, geese, cows, pigs, sheep, fish and others are slaughtered so we can eat.

I have raised many different kinds of chickens, ducks, geese, pheasants, quail, doves, pigeons, guinea fowl, sheep and goats. I have sometimes had to kill some of them to eat. I have also hunted and taken deer and wild ducks and other birds. To me, it is much more difficult to kill a bird or animal that I have raised than to kill a wild one that I have never known. The tame birds and animals have been with you, often since the day they were born. They have looked to you for protection and food. Then, when the time comes that they must be killed, it is a little sad.

If I, therefore, feel sadness that they must die so I can eat, I am sure that God feels the same. We were created in His image. I know the animals that I have raised, but God knows them even better than I do.

Is it wrong then to kill an animal to eat? No, because God Himself says that there are certain birds and animals that are for people to eat. In fact, the Bible says this in 1 Timothy 4: 1-5. Here it is talking about the day we are living in right now, and in verse 3 it says that people will be saying it is wrong to eat meats that God has created to be eaten. Now, many believe that verse 4 gives them the right to eat any and all creatures, but verse 5 says, *"For it (the kinds of creatures God has said are good) is sanctified by the word of God."* Sanctified means to "set apart". It also means "holy" kadosh or kosher, as most understand it. If you turn back to Leviticus Chapter 11, it tells you which birds and animals God says are good for humans to eat.

When I was younger, I ate everything I hunted. I ate raccoons, opossums, rabbits, squirrels, muskrats, frog legs, catfish and others. I loved catching big catfish in the spring and summer and I loved eating fried frog legs. I also loved the taste of barbequed pork ribs and crispy bacon. However, when I learned that God said I should not eat them I change my life. Not only did I have to quite eating these animals, I also had to give up hunting them. Most people, that follow eating only kosher, must just change their eating habits; but I had to change my entire life. It was I, however, that had asked God to show me the truth and once I found it, I could not turn my back on Him.

What has this to do about pets going to heaven? Some of the animals I have mentioned are animals that we eat every day for food, and yet some of these same animals are sometimes pets. In some countries, even dogs and cats are eaten. As I said earlier, all animals must die and it is much more humane for a deer or other animal to die quickly from being hunted than from slowly starving to death, dying of disease or being torn apart by a predator. The Bible says in Proverbs 12: 10 that a righteous man cares for the welfare and life of his animals.

At this point, I would like to interject something that many may not know. God is the one that told the Israelites of ancient times that they must kill or sacrifice animals to "cover" their sins.

When the priests, the ones responsible for the slaying of these many thousands of animals each year, killed them, they did it with mercy. The Bible says in Matthew 5:7 "Blessed are the merciful for they shall obtain mercy."

The priests would gently pet the animal that was to be killed and by using a very sharp knife, they would then cut the animal's throat. The knife was so sharp and the animal's mind was on the man petting it that it felt almost nothing. It then bled until it blacked out and its death was very humane. The animals also had no fear of humans as they were domesticated. They trusted people, for people had taken care of and provided for them all of their life. The Bible mentions this in Isiah 53:7 and the verse says, "as a lamb led to the slaughter, He opened not his mouth." This shows that we are to have mercy on animals, even if we do have to kill them. Animals share this earth with us and we need to have compassion on our fellow creatures. This is why a hunter should respect his prey and be a good marksman. He also needs to understand his quarry and not take a shot unless he knows he can make a clean and quick kill. This way, the death of the animal will be merciful.

In today's world, there are farms that crowd animals together so close that it is unhealthy for the animals and for the people that consume the meat produced by these animals. This should not be so. We must eat, but we need to treat the animals that give their lives so we can eat, respect.

While I am on the subject of being merciful to animals and the right or wrong of killing them, I would like to quickly bring up the title of this book again. The title is *Thou Shall Not Kill* and as I said, it really means the murder of an innocent human being. If we are concerned about the welfare and treatment of animals, we should be a hundred times more concerned with the treatment of children. Many people stand up for the cruelty of animals and there is nothing wrong in caring about animals, but what about an unborn human being that is ripped apart in the womb. Some are even being born with their heads out of the womb, but because they are not "completely born" yet they can be killed. This is murder! You can also rest assured that God will hold those responsible accountable. If you would like a poem that I wrote called *Condemned,* it is in several of my books including *My Favorite Poems*. I have also added it at the end of this book. Even though I have the copyrights, feel free to make and give away as many as you want. This poem has been published in the thousands and I know for sure that it has saved at least one baby's life.

Now back to the subject at hand. What about trapping, and the killing of animals this way? This is sometimes more controversial than hunting.

Traps for rats and mice snap down on the animal's head and usually kill then almost instantly. Many times, we have no choice in killing pests that carry disease and cause destruction to our crops or property.

There are many kinds of traps, and long ago, during the fur trade, leg hold traps were normally used to catch and hold animals. These leg-hold traps were used to catch many kinds of furbearing animals such as mink, muskrats, beaver and fox, among others. Today, they are not used as much and most trappers use traps that quickly drown the animals they catch in water. In America, game laws stipulate that traps must be checked every day. I myself do not trap. I have trapped nuisance animals alive, but as God said, a righteous man cares for the welfare of his beasts. I do not like to see anything suffer. Therefore, I personally do not think that a trap that causes pain and suffering should be used, except in rare situations. A rare case would be when a dangerous animal needs to be caught that could kill or injure someone and there is no other way to do it.

The world was different in the past, and it will be different in the future. What was done in the past is not necessarily what we should do today. No, it is not wrong to kill or trap an animal, if it is done humanely and for the right reason. Also, today, some people, whose children are hungry, kill many animals to sell or eat. Often it is the wealthy, which pays to have rare or endangered animals caught or killed, but it is the poor and needy that end up paying the highest price. This will someday end, but right now, the world is caught in a trap itself.

When I was young, I sometimes built a rabbit box trap to catch a rabbit alive. I never caught one, but I did catch an opossum and once I caught a young groundhog that I wanted for a pet.

Dead falls were often used in pioneer days for large animals such as bears, as was large log traps. They are rarely used today. Pits were also used in some countries to catch tigers, wild boar or other animals. Nets have been used since biblical days because the Bible speaks of a "fowlers net." It also mentions that nets were used, not only for birds and fish, but also for wild cattle and other animals. It says in Isaiah 51:20, that a wild bull in a net would be full of anger! I would think so.

Snares are another type of trap that has been used for animals for centuries. The Bible even speaks of the "time of trouble" coming upon the world as a snare. Today, in many countries, people use illegal snares with wire that catch, kill and maim animals, many of which are rare or endangered. A snare can cause an animal such as a chimp, gorilla or other to lose a hand or arm even if it survives. In addition, if a snare or other trap is not checked often, the poor animal (if it is alive) will suffer a long and agonizing death.

As a child, my father showed me how to make a snare to catch rabbits, but the only thing I ever caught was a possum. Today, I would never use one because there are several reasons snares are bad. One is that if an unwanted animal happens to get caught, it will most likely die. A snare usually is made for small game such as rabbits, but a dog or other animal could be caught in it. Another reason is that even if you catch the animal you want, it will die of strangulation. This means that it will not bleed and will die because it had no air to breathe. This is not a terrible way to die, but not a quick and merciful one either. God said that an animal should not be eaten if it has been strangled. It needs to be bled when it is killed. Almost any sportsman that hunts knows that when you kill an animal it needs to be bled so the meat will taste good. Therefore, if you do what He says, you would not kill and eat an animal this way.

God also says that *most species of animals are not good to eat*; therefore, they should not be killed for food. As said earlier, some animals such as mice, rats, or other pests, must be killed to stop disease or destruction of our food or property. Occasionally, some animals can become dangerous to humans and must be destroyed.

Today, however, many species face extinction because of man's greed. Elephants and rhinos are being killed for their tusks and horns. Every tusk and horn would someday be available when the animals die of natural causes. However, by killing them before they get a chance to reproduce, their population will keep going down until they are totally gone from the wild.

I was born, and lived most of my early life (until I was eleven), on Little Pigeon Creek, in Southern Indiana. As a child, I often wondered why the creek was called what it was because I never saw any pigeons near it. When I got older, I learned that long ago, millions of passenger pigeons once flocked along the creek's banks. Now the passenger pigeon is extinct, gone forever. Man's greed killed them all. The same goes for the Carolina parakeet and the ivory-billed woodpecker. Besides being killed for their meat, feathers or bills, their forests were cut down and they had nowhere to live.

I very much miss the passenger pigeon, the Carolina parakeet and the ivory-billed woodpecker.

The dodo bird, the giant moa, elephant bird and great auk are all gone, too, just because of man's greed and selfishness. I wish I could see them, but I never will in my lifetime, nor will anyone else, until God makes a new heaven and new earth. This is why I am writing this book. Is there any hope that we will someday get to see the pets and or the animals that have died? I will answer these questions in the following chapters.

Note: Again, much of this chapter is from *Do pets go to Heaven?* Therefore, I will not answer this last question in this book.

Chapter 14

Above is the spectacular male Golden Pheasant.

What Animals Should be Killed?

What animals should be killed and what animals shouldn't be? No animal should be killed that is so rare that it could cause it to go extinct. If God took the time to create it, He must have wanted it on the earth. Every animal has a place in the web of life.

Almost no one has a problem with killing a roach in their kitchen. Neither do they have much of a problem with the killing of a mouse or rat. We must sometimes destroy pests such as flies, mosquitoes and other harmful insects. Other times, we do not have much of a choice in killing larger pests. As I said earlier, recently there have been coyotes attacking children. I would not hesitate a second to kill a coyote if I saw it attacking or trying to attack a child, adult or even someone's pet. I have had to destroy opossums and raccoons that were killing my poultry. I have also raised baby raccoons and other animals because they needed help. As I said, we live in a world that is a paradox.

Many do not know that the whitetail deer was nearly gone from North America by the late 1800s, as were the beaver, otter, wild turkey, and others. Because of conservation efforts by hunters and other concerned people, they were brought back and reestablished where they once lived.

This came at a high cost and many do not know who paid for it. The Pittman-Robertson Federal Aid in Wildlife Restoration Act of 1937 was responsible for wildlife restoration in North America. This act was an excise tax on sporting arms, ammunition and fishing tackle. The funds derived from this tax (a tax that American sportsmen wanted) were used for research and the transplanting of the animals back into their former habitat.

Now we have so many deer that they are a problem in many areas. Tens of thousands are involved in automobile collisions every year. Deer eat people's trees and flowers in their yards (in my yard especially). Some have even attacked people. In other places, they have overpopulated and have eaten all available food and then have starved.

In days gone by, wolves, cougars and other predators killed deer and kept their population in check. Today, they must be hunted or they will die a slow agonizing death from starvation or disease. As I said in the proceeding chapter, that in Proverbs 12:10, a righteous man cares about the welfare of even animals. This is why I have a problem with those that would rather see an animal, such as a deer, slowly and painful die of starvation or disease instead of quickly dying from a hunter's bullet. They cannot care for the welfare of the animal.

The title of this book is *Thou Shall Not Kill*. This is the sixth Commandment that God gave mankind. I said before that it should read, "Thou shall not murder." Murder is the taking of an innocent human life. The two criminals on the cross beside Christ said in their own words that they deserved to die for what they had done. If a person must die for taking the life of an innocent person, it makes the value of life very high. If, on the other hand, they serve a short time in prison or get away with it, it makes human life cheap. Today, human life is getting cheaper and cheaper. This, however, is a different subject and I want to discuss animals.

Are there some animals that should never be killed? Yes, many. Earlier I said that most people would have no problem killing insects and mice, but what about higher animals? There is nothing wrong with taking the lives of the ones God that has "set apart" for eating, such as cattle, sheep, goats, deer and others that He says are good to eat. Wasting is another sin. It is a crime in America to kill a game animal and waste it. There are many hungry people, including children, and food should not be wasted.

There are higher forms of life such as the great apes, whales and others that should not be killed. They are not made for humans to eat and they are not harmful. In the jungles of South America, the natives sometimes must kill primates to eat. The Eskimos once had to often depend on seals and whales in order to survive. Some of them still hunt different animals to survive.

There is no reason, however, that a gorilla should ever be killed. Now days, neither should a whale or porpoise. In the past, people often needed products made from many of these animals. Today, however, this is not necessary. In days gone by, people did not also know how intelligent some of these animals were.

Many animals, such as elephants, were killed as food, but I believe they should not be killed unless they become dangerous to humans or are over populated and there is no other choice. They are too intelligent and God says they are not for human consumption.

This dilemma of the overcrowding of animals and the loss of their habitat has never happened before in the history of man. At the same time, we are learning that many of these animals are more important to us than we thought. All creatures are interconnected and each one needs the other to help keep the environment healthy. This is not only good for them, but also for us.

Many times, the available habitat that animals have is not enough and they destroy their own food sources. Some recent research suggests, however, that more elephants create more food sources by their normal behavior, thus causing more vegetation to grow.

Another problem today, is that much of the habitat is separated and now are just islands where interbreeding can be a problem.

Just as it is no problem for most of us to step on a roach or ant, it is more difficult to kill higher forms of life. I believe looking into the eyes of a gorilla, chimp or orangutan is nearly the same as looking into the eyes of a human. And to kill one with no reason other than for profit or anger would be right next to murder.

Now there is the question of killing animals in between these examples. What about bears, lions, wolves, or other large impressive animals that God said are not meant to be consumed by humans? Nowhere does God say that it is a sin to kill a lion, bear, tiger, or other such animal. He does say, however, that we should take care of the earth and that He will destroy those that destroy the earth. This should tell us that we need to be careful in how we act towards our fellow creatures. In days gone by, there were plenty of wild animals of all kinds and often it was necessary to kill them. Today, many are becoming rare and endangered. Some have already disappeared forever.

In the past, we were often at the mercy of animals, today they are at ours. As I have said, animals do not have a conscience and do not know good from evil, but we do.

Animals are programed to do what they do, we have free will.

Also, as I said earlier, every animal that is born must die. I can see nothing wrong (or not much) in taking the "excess animals" that will not contribute to the gene pool of their species if there are plenty of them. I do not care to kill a lion, but if there are several extra males or one is old and has no pride, I see nothing wrong in someone harvesting it before it dies a natural and sometimes painful death. The money from license fees and other money spent on the hunt will be used in protecting others of its kind, plus the habitat that the lion and many other species share.

Right as I was finished this book (July 2015), there was an incident that caused worldwide outrage. It was the killing of an African lion, named Cecil. I did not mention this incident in here originally, but I thought it should be. Was it wrong for this lion to be killed?

There is a story in the Bible in 2 Samuel 12, that answers this question. King David had just committed adultery with Uriah's wife and then had him killed by sending him into the "heat of the battle."

The story that Nathan the prophet told the king was this: There was a poor man and he had only one little lamb. This little lamb was like part of the family. It ate from the table and slept in the arms of the poor man and his family. It was like one of the children and was a part of the family. The poor man, however, worked for a rich man. One day, the rich man had some guests come for a big supper. The rich man had hundreds of sheep, but he sent and had the poor man's lamb slaughtered, dressed and served to his guests.

This story infuriated King David. He was a shepherd in his youth and he knew how this poor man and his family must have felt when their little pet lamb was killed, and for no good reason. King David even went so far as to say, "This man should be put to death!"

The moral of this story is that many in the world felt kinship to Cecil the lion. When he was killed just for the sake of putting a trophy on a wall, it infuriated people around the world. This is understandable. If this lion had attacked and killed someone, then it would have been a different story. The lion, however, was nearly like a pet, like the lamb in the story and was loved by many.

I do not know for sure if the gentleman that killed it was aware of who this lion was. He says he did not know. I am sure that the guides knew, but for thousands of dollars, people will do a lot of bad things. If the gentleman knew, then he should not have hunted the lion. In addition, if he knew that it was like a pet, he should not be allowed to hunt anything ever again.

This is a perfect example of what this book is addressing. It is the greed that has destroyed not only the creatures of the earth, but the earth itself. It was greed that destroyed the great auk. It was greed that killed hundreds of millions of passenger pigeons. Many of which were on nests trying to raise their young. In Deuteronomy 22:6-7 it says that you can take a young bird from its nest, but you have to let the female go. If this was done, the passenger pigeon would not have gone extinct.

The American bison or buffalo almost became extinct also. Our own government wanted them destroyed so the Native Americans would not be able to fight and would have to surrender. Still to this day, the bison does not run wild as do all other large game animals. Almost all herds are semi-domesticated.

Our country condemns other countries for destroying the rainforest, yet we destroy farmland. *Only one-half of one percent of the earth is tillable*. This is not *good land,* but land that can be tilled to grow even a marginal crop. If you go to the back of the Bible, it will tell you that one of the horsemen of the Apocalypse rides a black horse. This horseman on the black horse represents starvation. In the not too distant future, the world population will crash, the same as any other creature because we will not have enough food. War, disease and other natural disasters will also contribute to the food shortages and famines. We need to conserve land that will grow our food. It is the most valuable resource we have on the earth.

Now, back to the innocent of Cecil the lion. I saw something on line while this discussion about the lion was going on and I will say what it was in a moment. I can understand why people are upset about Cecil. Some subspecies of lions are already extinct. The Spanish lion is one. There are a few lions in captivity that have some bloodlines of the Spanish subspecies and someday there could be one bred that appears to be full-blooded, but where could it be free to run wild. It was the largest and most beautiful lion of all. The males had a black mane that went all the way down its chest onto its belly. From what I have seen of Cecil, he was a black mane lion and the most beautiful that roams wild at this time.

The point I wanted to make, however, was what I saw on the internet and what I mention in this book. I, along with many others, can understand why the killing of this lion outraged people. On the other hand, however, what about the thousands of premature babies that were killed the same day the lion was and dumped into a trashcan? This kind of killing is justified by most of the world and they call it abortion. This was the real reason God wrote the sixth commandment.

Chapter 15:

Do Animals Feel Emotions?

Above are Indian runner ducks and Embden geese. They have just been released from their pen and are excited to be free to roam the yard for a while.

I have raised several kinds of wild birds and animals, and many kinds of domestic ones as well. Besides dogs and cats, I've had the common kinds of poultry: ducks, geese, chickens, pigeons, doves, and Guinea fowl. I've also raised several kinds of wild birds and animals: crows, bobwhite quail, Gamble's quail, California quail, chukar partridge, ring-neck pheasants, Reeves pheasants, Lady Amherst pheasants, and Golden pheasants. In addition, I've raised sheep and goats.

Besides the common domestic birds and animals, I've raised wild animals such as: raccoons, cottontail rabbits, groundhogs, fox squirrels, flying squirrels, opossums, along with others such as snakes, lizards, and turtles of several kinds.

Besides these, I have rescued others and cared for them until they were able to make it on their own. I have raised several baby raccoons. Two of the ones I rescued have a book written about them, "Buddy and Rambo: The orphaned raccoons." They were also on local and national television and they have several videos on YouTube,

Most of the rest of this chapter is from my book "Do Pets Go to Heaven?" and I thought it should also be in this book:

All of us that have pets, or that have raised farm animals, seen animals in the wild or on television, know that animals have a range of emotional behavior. This photo above is an example of the joy animals feel when they are happy. The ducks and geese were just let out of their pen. I knew they would act this way because I had always released them from their pen each day, so they could have some freedom and eat grass in the yard. I had the camera ready and snapped several pictures. I had to keep them penned up for their own good because of all the predators that lived in the forest nearby. Predators such as: Mink, weasels, coyotes, foxes, raccoons, opossums, bobcats, eagles, hawks, and owls.

Every day that I went to let them out they would be crowding near the gate knowing what was about to happen. Then, as soon as the gate was open, they would run across the yard and beat their wings trying to get off the ground. The geese would honk and look at one another as if they were telling the others how good it felt to be free.

Anyone that has ever had a dog, knows how happy they are to see you after you've been a way awhile and come back home. My dog, Princess, used to wait by the window when it was time for the school bus to arrive in the afternoon. I do not know how she knew it was time for it, but she did. About five minutes before it was to arrive, she would sit there and wait. Then, when she heard the brakes of the bus being applied to stop the bus, her tail would begin to wag. Peeking out the window, she would watch the bus slow down, stop, and our two sons get off. She would then run to the kitchen door and wait until they came in. After greeting them, she would walk away and go back to her normal behavior.

Once, when my father came for a visit, he happened to notice that Princess' water bowl was about empty. Therefore, he went to the kitchen sink, filled her water bowl with water and gave it to her. All the time he did this he was talking to her saying things like, "The poor dog is out of water and no one will get her any." She wagged her tail in appreciation, then walked over and took a drink from her bowl. After that day, every time my father would come for a visit, she would meet him at the door. And as soon as she saw that it was him, she would go get her water bowl and carry it in her mouth, with water sloshing all over the floor, and try to give it to him. She wanted him to know that she remembered what he had done.

I remember reading a story once of a dog that loved his master so much, that when the old man died, the dog went and laid on top of the grave. Here he stayed, only leaving for short periods to eat. The dog stayed there on that grave for several years until he, too, died. People that knew about it were so impressed by the dog's loyalty, that they buried the dog beside his master.

When I had pygmy goats, they would often show joy in the evening as the summer sun went down. It would be cooler then and they would run, jump, kick up their heels and play with one another. They would jump on something, such as a stump, and play "king of the hill" and try to butt one another off. You could easily see that they were feeling joy and happiness.

Animals also have fear. We see this all the time when they run from us or a predator. God had to put it in them for their own survival. They also feel anger. Just give two strange dogs a bone and see what happens. Anger is there to keep other males from mating with the dominate male's females. It is also there to help assure that the animal will have enough to eat.

In the world now, it is literally dog eat dog. Many species of birds and animals seem cruel in the way they behave. Often, if they have too many young to care for, they will let some of them die. This is to ensure that the others live. Even nestlings will often kill one another if there is not enough food. House sparrows and European starlings were imported over here to America and if they can evict woodpeckers or purple martins from their nests, they will. They will even toss out the young to let them die. The same goes for parasitic birds such as the European cuckoo or the brown-headed cowbird here in America. In the future, all this will change and animals will be at peace with one another.

My pygmy goats

Chapter 16

Above is a beautiful male wood duck. Photo by
Indiana Wildlife Photographer, Joe Williams.

An Electrifying Duck Hunt

In this section, I wanted to put a few stories from my
book "Barnestorming the Outdoors: Revised edition." Some
are humorous and some show how some of the Native
Americans thought of the animals they hunted for food.

It was a Saturday evening in November of 1968. My
friend John had just called and told me that right before
dark, in a field near his house, there had been a flock of
geese and a couple hundred ducks land to spend the night. I
had heard of geese roosting in fields, but never ducks.
"Are you sure?" I questioned.
"Yeah," he answered. "I can hear them from here."

This I had to see. The next day was Sunday, and in 1968, hunting on Sunday was not allowed. So late in the afternoon of the following day, I arrived at John's, picked him up in my dad's old truck, and parked on the side of a gravel road near the field.

"It was about sunset when they came yesterday," John said as we sat there staring out over the field.

I still could not believe it, but sitting in the truck waiting, I was full of excitement. I could see them in my mind: *Two hundred mallard ducks cupping their wings and gliding down towards me. I could also see the flash of iridescent green on the drakes' heads—dozens of them as they begin landing all around me. And I could hear the hens' loud calls as they came in with the males. So many to choose from I would have difficulty knowing which ones to shoot first. Then with the blast of the shotgun, there would be a mighty rushing sound of wings as they beat the air, trying to get back into the sky. I would be smiling as I began walking out to pick up my limit of ducks. Then, when I picked up the last one, I suddenly would hear the unmistakable sound of Canada geese honking in the distance. I would again take my place in the blind and repeat everything, except this time with the giant geese.*

It looked so good in my mind, but was it true? Would there be any coming tonight, or did John dream it? I had already bought my hunting license and duck stamp. At home, I had plenty of high-powered shells with number 4-shot—I was all set. Now all I needed were the ducks and the geese.

Soon I would have my answer, for it was getting close to sunset.

"This was about the time they came last night," John said.

Looked out the window with anticipation, I still saw nothing. "Are you sure it was this field?"

"Yeah, they were right here," John assured.

74

Staring out over the field, I saw a small flock of blackbirds heading for their roost, but no ducks and sadness began to creep into my heart.

"There they are, I think," John said, interrupting my feeling of sinking disappointment.

"Where?" I replied searching the sky.

"Over there," he said, pointing to a dark mass of large birds far to my left and about a half mile away.

"That's ducks!" I said keeping my eyes glued to the horizon.

As we watched, the ducks kept coming closer and closer until they were over the field. They then began circling the field as I rolled down the truck window to get a better view. We could hear them quacking as they continued circling several times before landing about a hundred yards out in the field.

"I never would have believed it if I hadn't seen it," I told John. No geese showed up, but the excitement of seeing a hundred and fifty to two hundred ducks landing in a bare cornfield was enough for me.

"We'll be here tomorrow waiting for them," I said, starting the truck to take John home.

The next day at school, John and I discussed our planned hunt. We would have to be there in plenty of time before they arrived to build a blind, and it had to be tomorrow. The ducks were on their way south and could leave at any time. Also, the corn left in the field after harvesting may soon be gone too. Opportunities like this didn't happen very often, so we would have to take advantage of it.

As soon as I got home that afternoon, I quickly changed, ate a bite, and rushed over to John's. He was ready by the time I arrived and a few minutes later, we were at the field.

Getting out of the truck and walking to the field, I noticed something I hadn't the evening before. The farmer who owned the field had put up an electric fence so he could turn his hogs loose to clean up any corn left on the ground. I hadn't seen any hogs yesterday, they must have been at the other end of the field or maybe the farmer hadn't brought them in yet. They were nowhere to be seen, so they wouldn't be a hindrance.

I did, however, see one small problem—what to make a blind out of? After talking it over with John, we had little choice than try and gather corn stalks and see if we could build a large enough blind to conceal us both. We didn't discuss this, however, until we had both stepped over the electric fence and were inside the pen.

The field was very muddy from a recent rain, and our shoes had already gathered huge clods of mud on them.

Looking around, we saw a few corn stalks, but most were scattered outside the pen along the edge of the field. There was also some tall grass growing along a ditch that bordered the field that we could use.

"I'll get the corn stalks and throw them over the fence and you can make the blind," John said.

That sounded good, and it would cut down on the time it took us to build it. Things had gone pretty smooth up until now, but I should have known by then, that an adventure with John never went smooth.

Approaching the fence, John stopped, and I could see that he might have a problem getting over it. As he stood there looking at the small wire that was about two feet off the ground, I could tell he was studying the best way to proceed.

"How are you going to get over?" I asked.

"I'm going to jump," he answered with a little uncertainty.

"I would try and step over it if I were you," I cautioned.

"I can make it," he replied with confidence.

Standing a short distance away, I was watching and wondering if he could clear it or not. I knew it would be difficult to jump the fence with all that heavy mud clinging to his size 14 shoes, because by now, each shoe had a clump of mud on them about the size of a basketball. There was no way to get a run at the fence in the muddy field, so he would have to make it in one leap, while standing still. I was a little apprehensive as he left the ground, and for good reason. As he jumped, one foot made it over, but the other failed to clear the electric wire. Suddenly John was standing straddle of the fence. He was also beginning to sink in the gooey mud, which caused the wire to slowly inch up towards his crotch!

I could tell by the shocked, confused look on his face that he didn't know which way to go or what to do. I once saw a dog become tangled in an electric fence, and it wasn't a pretty sight. Suddenly I was lost in deep thought:

I remember it was a calm, quiet, hot summer afternoon, and I was trying to sneak up on some pigeons that were feeding in a hog pen, next to a field, that bordered a large woods. A hog pen that my landlord owned.

Being a hot day, the pigs (all two hundred head) were peacefully lying on their sides dozing in the shade as I came upon them. The dog, which was out ahead of me, started for the electric fence. Softly I began calling the not too bright canine, trying to keep him away from the danger. I was also trying not to spook the sleeping hogs or any pigeons that might have been feeding. The stupid dog, however, kept going towards the fence and paying me no mind. He was just fine as he lowered himself and began crawling under the wire. At least he was fine until the hot wire reached his tail. Then, like a clap of thunder the peace and quiet was suddenly shattered and utter chaos erupted! The crazed dog began yelping at the top of his lungs. Then he turned, bared his teeth and began snarling and snapping at the wire that was causing him such agony. Instantly I saw all of the pigs' eyes flash open in fear, as they were jarred awake. The panicked animals then grunted, squealed, and jumped to their feet. Instantly thy began a mad stampede through the woods, which caused a thick cloud of dust to billow up that soon obscured my view of the confused, terrified animals. All the while, the frightened dog continued yelping and nipping at the wire, trying to get free of the biting fence. It reminded me of the herd of swine in the Bible that was set upon by a thousand demons that rushed down a hill and plunged to their death in the sea. I thought for sure that the startled pigs would break through the fence and drown in the creek, or at least be scattered through the six hundred acres of woods, which would be very difficult to explain to my landlord. It was a little more excitement than I wanted for one day.

Waking from my daydream I looked over at John, who was still trying to escape his predicament. He was not yelping, snarling, or snapping at the wire, but he was baring his teeth, and he did look a little crazed as he was making some very odd moaning sounds. He was also dancing around a lot, as the wire jostled between his legs. All I could do was watch and grimace as he lifted one mud clogged foot, then the other, trying to get free. It took him awhile to get off the fence and I guess it felt like an eternity to him as the hot wire bit one inner thigh then the other, as he kept sinking deeper in the mud. Finally, however, he was able to get one leg over the wire thus ending his torment. Then after making some unprintable comments about the fence, we continued our construction of the duck blind.

At last, it was finished and we took our place inside. John had recovered sufficiently from his unfortunate experience, and we were looking forward for the arrival of the ducks. They would arrive just a few minutes before sunset, but that would be long enough to bag our limit before they wised up and left the field.

Standing there in the mud, we kept searching the empty sky as minute by minute ticked away until the sun was going down. And as you probably have already guessed, no ducks ever showed up.

All the planning, the work, everything we had done, and all of John's pain and suffering had been in vain. That's the way it always seemed to go. We never went back, and the ducks never returned to the field. I do, however, have the memories of a duck hunt that I shall never forget, and I doubt neither will John.

Chapter 17

Above is me with my first deer that I took with a muzzle loading rifle. The rifle was a .45 caliber Kentucky rifle that I put together from a kit.

Why Have a Primitive Weapons Season?

The whitetail deer were extinct in my state of Indiana after 1893, and were absent or nearly so from many other Midwestern states. Then in the 1930s deer were transplanted from states where they were plentiful to states where they were rare or absent. Once they were protected their numbers began a steady increase and by the early 1950s many states began a limited hunting season.

When the whitetail deer began to multiply in our country after many years of decline, many sportsmen took to the field to hunt the most popular big game animal in North America.

Early settlers as well as Native Americans hunted the deer for food and for its soft durable skin. Soon after the first modern-day deer seasons began primitive weapons seasons were established. Why have a season where you are "handicapped" with the use of weapons used 150 to 200 years ago? We have modern guns capable of rapid fire, fitted with scopes and accurate enough to put every shot into an apple-sized target at 200 or even 300 yards. So why on earth would you want to use a gun that you have to load from the muzzle and use a patched ball or greased bullet? Why would you want to use black powder which bellows out a cloud of smoke that obscures your target until the wind blows it away; powder which also corrodes the inside of your gun barrel unless you scrub it with hot water and soap? Why use percussion caps that may not fire it they get wet or that might fall off the nipple, or use a stone made of flint that might fail to set off the priming powder?

And why would anyone hunt with the most primitive of weapons, two sticks and a string, the weapon the Native Americans used? They would do it because it is a challenge and because of our pioneer heritage. It is to see and feel as our ancestors did in a new country and wilderness of long ago.

Today it seems that few understand this. Today, nearly everyone wants to get a little more "edge." Why? Where shoguns only are allowed, there are shotguns with scopes and fully rifled barrels, using sabot slugs, which can group the shots less than two inches apart at one hundred yards. They can also fire five or six shots without reloading. Moreover, in many states, a center fire rifle can be used that can take deer at 300 yards or more.

On the market now are "modern" muzzle loading rifles. They have thumb hole stocks, an in-line firing system, are drilled and tapped for telescopic sights, have prepackaged pellet propellant, can shoot jacketed hollow point bullets and group the shots under an inch at one hundred yards. When you pull the trigger on a deer, that first shot is not much different than shooting a modern center fire rifle.

Some states are beginning to restrict their use. There is no reason not to use the modern muzzleloaders during regular gun season. You want the most accurate gun possible in taking a deer, but during a special primitive weapons season I believe most are missing the very reason we have it.

Back in the early 1970s, I first recall compound bows. My friend Mike had one and came over one day to shoot with me. The bow looked strange with pulleys and cables all over it. I shot it a few times at the target, but it felt unnatural.

Back then, many people had difficulty holding a bow at full draw, especially on deer that were just not in the right position to shoot. I remember feeling sorry for the wimpy men who could not hold back a fifty or sixty-pound pull bow. Now as I'm entering my senior years and pulling back a compound bow that has been cranked up to 80 pounds or more makes me feel wimpy. However, I still feel the same and I only shoot a recurve.

On bows today, there are overdraws which shoot ultra-light carbon arrows and bows that shoot faster and flatter by having peak draw weights of 80 pounds or more. Fred Bear, the father of modern-day archery, only used a 65-pound recurve to take all game he hunted—from deer to grizzly bear to elephant.

The bows are so heavy today with stabilizers, telescopic or laser sights, sight lights, sight guards, kisser buttons, over draws and string silencers that you need to wear a bow holder to carry one. And to shoot it, most now use a hand-held release. If something breaks, the shooter is usually left helpless.

The recurve or longbow is a beautiful work of art, one piece with a string on it, how simple. No pulleys to break, no "cranking" it up or down, no telescopic sights to worry about, just pull it back and shoot.

My first bow (at age 12) I tried to make myself. After three days of whittling a piece of hickory, I had it completed. After a few more days of letting it cure, I got impatient and wanted to shoot it. The first time I pulled it back at full draw it cracked.

My first "real" bow I got that Christmas, an "Ol' Hickory" bow made by Ben Pearson. It was a 30-pound wooden recurve with cedar arrows. I hunted groundhogs, rabbits, squirrels, frogs, and even tried to shoot crows as they flew over (but they would dodge my arrows).

Many or most have not even shot a recurve or longbow. Today the compound is accepted as being the "norm." Some who have used the compound have switched to the "traditional" recurve or longbow for the "extra challenge." Isn't that the whole point in having a "primitive" weapons season?

Chapter 18

Hunting in the Fourth Dimension

My first buck did not come easy; it actually took years. When I first began deer hunting, I was but fifteen; that was in 1966. Back then, deer were rather scarce, with only about 5,000 killed annually throughout the entire state of Indiana. The seasons were very short, with only antlered bucks being legal. In addition, places where deer were plentiful enough to hunt weren't always close. On top of this, the guns to hunt them with were far less effective than they are today. There were no slug guns with rifled barrels or rifle sights, let alone scopes. The best gun at the time or shortly thereafter, which I knew nothing of, was *Ithaca's Deerslayer*. Even if I knew of it, I could not have afforded one. The gun I had to use was even less desirable than a regular one. All I had in those days was a 16-gauge H&R single-shot. It had a 26-

inch cylinder bore barrel because the previous owner had shortened it by two inches. Because of this, it didn't even have a front sight. It did shoot consistently, however— about a foot low at 30 yards. Not the best gun to bag a buck with, but my enthusiasm was high as was my energy. I walked many miles and waited many hours with not so much as a glimpse of a buck.

Several years later, I was still trying for my first deer. Every season I had high hopes of bagging one. The population was beginning to grow and deer were moving into new areas, areas closer to home. The yearly harvest had doubled, but still, by today's harvest it was but a tiny fraction. My chances, however, were improving. I had learned a lot in all that time. I had studied deer sign; read all I could about them, and was in the field as much as possible.

Deer had now moved into a very large woods right behind my house, and their numbers were increasing. I also had a slug barrel on my Remington 870 12-gauge *Wingmaster* pump shotgun. It was fairly accurate, so all I needed now was to spot a buck close enough for a shot.

That year was going to be *my* year. I knew the woods like my backyard, for it was. I knew where the deer traveled, what they ate, and where they bedded down. So as the season approached, I was ready. Then, as my luck usually goes, I became very ill with the flu, which led to some serious infections, causing me to miss the first week of the season. I knew the majority of deer killed during the season are taken during the first weekend, and my hopes went down.

Before the season began, I had scouted out the area and found plenty of deer sign. One area in particular looked very good. My 14-year-old cousin, Paul, had accompanied me on the last scouting trip and we discovered several rubs. We also saw a scrape and I surmised that the buck was in the area a lot.

After checking the size of the trees the buck had rubbed, and the size and depth of his tracks, I knew it wasn't a huge deer, but I knew it wasn't a small one either.

"You think it's a big one?" Paul asked looking down at the tracks, I was examining.

"He's not bad," I answered, rising up from where I was squatting. "I would guess he'd go about 175 pounds and is about an eight pointer." Then hesitating and joking, I added, "No, a seven pointer, he's had one broken off."

Paul looked at me smiling. "A seven pointer?"

"Yeah," I said with a grin.

In the middle of the second week of the season, I was feeling better, but still weak and running a slight fever every now and then. I tried to rest as much as possible, and on the morning that I decided I would try to go, I awoke late and it was already getting light. It was a dark and gloomy day, with a light mist of rain falling. It was a good day for deer to be moving.

Putting on a green lightweight rain suit, I grabbed my hunter orange hat so I'd be legal and went to the gun cabinet. I decided to take my 20-gauge double-barreled shotgun. I had tested it and knew exactly where each barrel shot. The right barrel shot a little high and to the left; the left barrel shot right exactly where I aimed. I didn't feel like carrying the heavier 12-gauge, besides, I thought my chances of seeing a deer were slim. I figured the deer that had been making all the rubs and scrapes, was venison in someone's freezer by then.

Walking slowly through the woods, I kept an eye out for any movement until I had gone about a half mile. I was now in the area where I'd seen all the deer sign two weeks before.

Coming to a ridge, I saw a small trail that deer had been using to come and go and figured this would be a good place to sit and wait. On this ridge, I could see two valleys, one to my left and one to my right, and a ridge on either side of the valleys. I would be watching the entire side of the southwestern part of the hill where the deer had been coming.

Looking around, I didn't see much cover, but in front of me was a three-foot sapling with honeysuckle vines on it. Breaking the top down to give me a denser bush in which to hide behind, I sat down with my back against a large oak tree and waited.

The misty rain had nearly stopped, but the air was foggy and damp. I was thinking how good it was to be in the woods again, but wishing I would have been able to have hunted at the beginning of the season.

I sat there for perhaps twenty minutes, alternating between watching the ridge to my left and to my right. Suddenly in the distance, I heard a shotgun blast. It sounded like it was about a quarter of a mile away and to the west. It wasn't the hollow sound of a rifled slug. "Must be a rabbit hunter," I thought. "Maybe he'll spook a deer this way."

I became even more alert, as I began looking for any movement and listening for any sound.

About two minutes passed, when I thought I heard something. It sounded like a muffled rustling of leaves, but the leaves were still very wet and I strained to see what was making the noise. "Probably a squirrel searching for an acorn," I thought, looking to my left, then to my right. "I don't see anything. Must have been my imagination." But as I looked straight ahead, I saw something. On the other side of the tiny tree, I had broken over to help conceal me and through the vines that covered it, I saw two large eyes!

Staring at the large dark eyes that were looking at me, I saw an ear twitch. Then I started seeing an image appear and take shape as I saw an antler, then another. The buck had his head lowered and was looking at me less than ten feet away. I didn't dare move. I was sitting with my back against the tree and with my legs sticking straight out, my gun lying across my lab. Both hands were resting on the top of the gun as my heart began to race. "If only I'd seen him coming, I could have been ready," I thought. We both looked at one another, each afraid to make a move. "What if he charges?" went through my mind. "I've heard of bucks being aggressive during the rut. I'd be penned against this tree and there is no way I could raise the gun quickly enough before he covered the few feet that separated us."

"One wrong move and the deer will bolt and it will be very difficult to get a shot." Then, ever so slowly, I inched my finger toward the trigger and my thumb to the safety. Reaching the safety with my thumb, I carefully slid it off. I felt a little better. My finger was on the trigger and it was ready to fire. "Should I try and swing the gun in front of me and shoot before he moves?" He was so close, but the little sapling was directly in front of me. And I knew if I quickly swung the gun towards him, the gun barrel would hit it and bounce back, maybe causing me to miss. I had to keep cool or I'd miss my chance at my first buck, and I still had my left hand on top of the barrels. "If only I hand my hand under the forearm, I wouldn't be afraid to try and shoot from the hip. Maybe he will walk away slowly, or turn his head so I can get my hand in the right position. Then, if his head is turned, I can quickly mount the gun and take an easy shot."

We both were frozen, but I had to make a move. So ever so slowly, I began moving my left hand, trying to get it under the forearm. As I barely moved my finger, I saw the deer begin to get nervous. Raising his head, he glanced to the left, then to the right. "He's trying to figure the best way to make his escape," I thought.

Suddenly he reared back! "This is it. He's going to bolt!"

Half a second later, he was taking off at full speed.

Sitting on the ground, with my legs stuck out and trying to jump to my feet was not easy, especially while holding a gun. I knew I had to shoot fast before he got away.

Struggling to my feet, I kept my eyes on the deer, but all I could see was a gray blur as he streaked passed me through the woods.

"He's only a few feet away," I thought, "I have to try a shot!" Pointing the gun towards the streak of gray, I pulled the trigger, expecting him to go down, but to my surprise, the deer kept going.

"Man, oh man!" I thought. "My first chance and I messed up!"

Turning towards him as he sped through the woods, I mounted the gun. He was about thirty yards away now and running at full speed through the trees and I was wishing I'd been ready when I first saw him. "I only have one shot left. I have to make it count."

Sighting down the barrel, I got the bead on the buck. Then, just as I was about to slap the trigger, he came to an abrupt halt and then turned around facing me! He must have been curious and turned to look at the odd creature wearing the green rain suit and orange hat. Here was my chance at long last. Finally, I had a clear shot at a buck. I had but one shot. This time, however, it was the left barrel, the one that was accurate. "Hurry, before he runs again," I told myself. "And make sure you don't miss!"

Quickly I moved the front sight to the base of his neck where his chest begins. "Now!" I said pulling the trigger.

Instantly the silence was again shattered as the blast sent the slug towards the buck, and just as quickly, the deer collapsed to the ground.

Grabbing two slugs from by pocket, I slipped them in the gun and began walking towards the deer, on the ready in case he tried to get up.

Nearing the buck, I saw he was kicking and I knew it was over. Reaching into my pocket, I took out my deer tag as I watched the deer. I had not been nervous until then, but now my hands were trembling. I knew I had to be cool or maybe miss the shot, but now it was over and I had my first buck.

The deer was beautiful, as I looked him over. "How many points does he have? Six, seven, eight; no, the eighth is broken off." Then the words I had spoken to my little cousin came running through my mind. He looked like he would weigh about what I said, too. In fact, when I weighed him, he tipped the scales at 175 pounds. To say the least, I felt strange. My prophetic joke had come true and as I was pondering this, I began thinking about the animal that I had just killed.

I had hunted a long time to take this buck. I had spent many seasons and many cold hours sitting in a blind waiting for a chance at a buck. I had learned his ways and had come to admire him.

As I looked him over, I could see that he was a magnificent creature, a creature that Indiana had lost and regained. He was designed to live in the woods, the woods that I was so fond of roaming. His gray fur blended in perfectly with the dead leaves that littered the forest floor. I also noticed his tail. When lowered, it hid the white underneath they often show when alarmed. His legs were strong to allow him to run and leap without much effort; his eyes able to see in the darkness; and his ears to hear the slightest sound. He was a marvelous animal, and I could not help but to feel some sadness. The woods seemed so empty now. I knew he would never travel its hills and valleys again, nor would I get to pit my cunning at trying to outwit him. I had won this time and he had lost, but he indeed was a worthy opponent.

I knew he had probably fathered more of his kind and they would be there to take his place, but I still felt the loss of him. It was then that I understood how the Native Americans felt about their world. They had reverence for the animals they hunted. They held the creatures the Great Spirit had made in high esteem, for they depended on these animals to give them life and the animals had their respect and admiration.

Today, some only see a deer or other game animal in two dimensions, a target to shoot. These are not sportsmen or even hunters. Many see the same animal in three dimensions, an animal they enjoy hunting and one they take pride in bringing home. Then there are others who see them in another dimension. They feel a kinship with the animals they hunt. They have respect and even fondness for a fellow creature that shares this same speck of dust in the universe. They take pride in hunting and even bringing game home, but they feel joy just being out in the woods and fields with the animals they are pursuing. They have a spiritual feeling towards them. They, like many others before us, hunt in the fourth dimension.

Chapter 19

In Memory of a Friend

When I lived in Warrick County, I was very close to the Ohio River. In fact, I could walk to Cypress Creek, which was literally in my back yard, get in a boat, and in less than ten minutes be there. Back then, I often hunted ducks on the river and I needed a retriever. Therefore, in the late summer of 1975, my friend, John, called me because he had seen an ad in the paper about a man close by selling black lab puppies. That same day I called the man and drove over to check them out.

When I arrived, three of the pups were playing in the yard. As I spoke with the gentleman, I learned that their father was a field trial champion. When I walked near the pups to try to choose one, I clapped my hands and stomped my foot. I did this to make sure none of them would likely be gun shy or afraid of me. Two of the pups stopped playing and looked at me, but one came running up to me, so it was she that chose me. I took her home that day and named her, Princess.

It was less than three months before duck season opened and I didn't believe I could teach her all that she needed to know so we could hunt that first season. She was so smart, however, that she didn't need much training. The first day we went duck hunting, she was only 4 ½ months old and she sat at my side in the blind looking out over the river and ready to do what she was born for.

The first duck, I shot that morning, fell about 50 yards out into the river. But on the command of "fetch," Princess leaped into the water, swam out, retrieved the duck and swam back to shore. She then sat before me holding the bird in her mouth until I took it from her. She had performed as if she had done this all her life.

Over the years, we hunted hundreds of times together. Sometimes we hunted woodcock, doves or quail. Once I downed a quail, which fell into some honeysuckle vines. Princess went to retrieve it but it had disappeared. She kept telling me by her actions that it was there, so I cleared all the vines out of the way and she reached down under the leaves and picked it up from below ground where it had hidden.

Sometimes while we were in the field, she would see a dove fly overhead and she would watch it fly by, then turn and look up at me as if to say, "Hey, didn't you see that?" She would also have a puzzled look as if to ask, "Why didn't you shoot?" Of course, she did not understand anything about hunting seasons and that doves were not legal game at that time.

Every night, she would lie on the rug beside my bed while I slept. Sometimes, however, she would sneak off and get on the couch, which she knew was against the rules. Then when she would hear me get up, she would jump off the couch so I would not catch her, but of course I saw the big depression in the cushion and I could feel the warm spot where she had been lying.

I remember once, when the kids were sledding down the hill behind our house, that the sled went out onto the frozen creek. The ice was too dangerous for a person to walk on, but with her four legs to disperse her weight it was a lot safer. The water was not that deep there either. Therefore, I sent her out to fetch it. With tail wagging, she went out and dragged the sled back to shore.

Another time I was cutting firewood and carrying it up the same hill and Princess wanted to help, so each time I carried an arm load of wood I handed her a piece, and again, with tail wagging she would carry it up the hill beside me.

During her ninth year, she became ill and I knew I would not have her much longer. At one time, she could climb a six-foot wooden fence when we crossed a field behind the house. I remember another time she actually dove under the water to retrieve a wounded duck. But the last time we had went hunting, I had to lift her over a three-foot fence, the same fence she used to easily leap over.

The last days of her life, I got up one morning and she was lying on the couch. As I came into the room, she looked up at me and in her eyes; I could see what she was asking. She was asking, "Is it alright if I stay on the couch and rest because I don't feel very good?" I removed the cushion and made her a bed on the couch, because now the rules did not matter.

A week before she died, I wrote a poem for her. As I sat on the bed that day, she sat on the rug beside me. She looked up at me as I told her that I had written a poem about her and that many people would hear it and she would always be remembered. As we sat looking at one another, with tears in my eyes, I read her, her poem. The poem is on the next page. The photo of Princess was taken overlooking Cypress Creek.

Chapter 20

Princess

This is written in memory of a friend who shared a part of my life. / She was just a tiny puppy the day I brought her home to the kids and my wife.

We were in the woods, the fields, and on the river when the cold winds blew. / We were under the autumn sky and we were in the early morning dew.

For nine years, she was a companion, who was at my side. / And I will never forget the look in her eyes the day that she died.

Because she knew, we would never again hunt the woodcock, the duck, or the dove. And I knew she didn't want to leave her master, her master whom she loved.

Princess, I will miss you in the morning by my bedside where you laid. / But I will never forget the memories, all the memories that we made.

And when I see a dove streak across the sky, I will think of you. / I'll remember your watchful eyes, and the sky won't seem as blue.

I shall never forget you my friend, for you will always be missed. / This is written in remembrance of you, farewell, my special, Princess.

Chapter 21

The Beauty of the Wild

(An excerpt from Life Along Little Pigeon Creek)

Nearly every day I was in the woods and fields, roaming, exploring, and learning new things. I loved the outdoors and all that it contained. I just couldn't get enough of being in the home of all the wild creatures. Besides being in it, I wanted to be a part of it. I wanted to touch it, taste it, and feel it. I liked to feel the wind blowing on me like it did on the tall, stately trees. I wanted to touch it, by being there with it. I also wanted to see it, by searching for all its wonders and secrets. I even wanted to taste it. I loved smelling the air after a summer shower and the flowers in the woods in the spring. Even the smell of the lake and pond had a good smell, like the wilderness itself. When I brought something home, like wild mushrooms, the big turtle, or bullfrogs and ate them, then the wilderness became a part of me and I a part of it. It made me feel kinship with nature and I often felt like one of my heroes, Davy Crockett.

That is why I loved going frog hunting. Besides, it let me escape from "the thorn in my side," my little brother, Thomas.

"Mommy, I'm goin' frog hunt'n," I said, as I started out the door with my trusty BB gun in hand.

Walking across the yard and down the hill into the woods, I was thinking about the giant frog I'd seen earlier that week. I had seen the huge frog sitting in the edge of the little pond that was just inside the woods, below our yard, but I hadn't seen him since.

Reaching the pond, I began looking for the big frog, walking very carefully all the way around the pond, but he was nowhere to be found.

"Maybe he has moved to the lake," I thought, so I went up the hill and back farther into the woods to the big lake to try my luck there.

After a while of stalking the edge of the lake without finding him, I gave up and headed back home.

Coming down the last little hill, the pond came back into view. When it did, out of the corner of my eye, to my left, I saw something move.

Stopping, I stood to see something I had never seen before. I looked just in time to see a large, beautiful, snow-white bird, with a long neck and long black legs, leap into the air from a log in the center of the pond.

With the woods surrounding the pond, the white bird contrasted sharply with the green foliage behind him. I watched as the magnificent bird gracefully rose higher and higher into the air, climbing until he cleared the tops of the trees. It then turned in the air and disappeared behind them.

Standing there, I kept staring into the empty blue sky where it had been. Now it seemed like it had never really happened, as if it was only a dream. I had never seen such a beautiful and graceful wild bird. Like a vision, it was there for a few short seconds, then it vanished and was gone forever.

Chapter 22

Cypress Creek where the incident took place.

A Cry for Help?

This is a story I wrote and have published in my book "Barnestorming the Outdoors: Revised edition. This story also gives one of the reasons I wrote this book.

One day, while in my backyard, I heard a strange noise. It was coming from near the creek a few yards from my house. At the time, I lived on Cypress Creek, near the Ohio River in Warrick County, which is in Southern Indiana. The creek was at the bottom of a hill behind my house, and I had cleared and mowed all the way to the water, so I would have a good place to fish.

As I stood there listening, I didn't know what could be making the unusual sound. It wasn't a bird or an insect, and it didn't sound like any animal I had ever heard before. The sound was a high-pitched *cry*. Being interested in nature since childhood, I was curious as to what was making the odd sound, so I went to investigate.

Nearing the creek, I followed the sound and soon saw something move in the short grass a few feet from me. There was a crayfish hole about eight or ten feet from the water, and at the entrance, I saw the source of the noise. A small leopard frog was half in the hole and half out; but why was he making the crying sounds? Suddenly he moved, and I saw the reason. He was being held tightly in the jaws of a garter snake. The snake was in the crayfish tunnel with his head just visible. The frog's hind legs were in the snake's mouth as the snake was trying to swallow him.

Looking down at the poor frog, I couldn't help but have compassion on it. It would be a terrible way to die, to be slowly swallowed alive and then to succumb to the burning acid in the darkness of the snake's belly.

The little frog continued to cry, as I searched for a stick.

Returning to the hole, I held the snake's head with the stick and freed the frog. I am sure that the snake was disappointed, but I'm also sure the frog was greatly relieved, as he hopped towards the water, jumped in and dove to the safety of the bottom.

After the incident, I began to reflect on it. Why did the frog cry out? Was it fear? Was it pain? Was it a cry for help? I have been on earth for nearly seventy years, and have spent countless hours in the woods and along streams and I've never heard a frog *cry* like that before. As a child, I loved hunting bullfrogs. I've killed hundreds of them; cleaned them, and fried their legs. All the times they were killed, not once did one cry out. In biology class during high school, I saw many frogs killed by a slow painful insertion of a pin to the brain, and not once did one make a sound.

So why did this one cry out? It was not that painful, for he was just being held by the snake, and even if it was, they don't cry out if hurt. It could have been fear; but the countless frogs I've seen die slowly must have known they were dying and never cried out. Was it then a cry for help? If so, why would a frog cry for help? No other frogs would or could come and rescue him. Birds give a warning cry when they see a snake, and other birds of many species will come and try to drive the snake away. The young of many animals and birds cry for their mother's help when afraid or in danger. Mother animals will often attack or try to lead a predator away. Some birds even "pretend" to be injured to lead an animal away from its young. Often, however, when a bird or animal does cry, it will bring predators. Nearly every kind of frog, however, lays its eggs in water and never sees their young again. On the other hand, when an animal does cry, predators often hear it and come so they can get an easy meal.

After thinking on it for a while, I came to the conclusion that it *was* a cry for help; not for its mother; not for others of its kind; but it was a cry for help from God.

Why would a frog or any creature cry for help when there is none? God will not reach down and save an animal that is the food of another. The reason is given in the Bible, which I will soon discuss.

Chapter 23

The Fatted Calf

This is a story from the Bible and one that I have slightly revised from my book, *Christ: His Words, His Life* and I wanted to put it at the end of the book. This is a famous story that the Lord told about how God loves us and it also talks about animals being killed to eat. Therefore, I thought it fit well into this book.

Then He (Christ) told them another parable, saying, *"There was a certain man that had two sons. The younger son came one day to his father and said, 'Father, give me the things of my inheritance.'*

"His father divided his money and property and gave to his son what was coming to him.

"Not many days later, the younger son gathered all that was his and went on a long journey into a far country. Now while he was there, he wasted all his money and goods on parties, women and drinking.

"After he ran out of money, there came a terrible famine in the land, and he began to go hungry; for all his 'friends' were nowhere to be seen.

"Soon afterwards, he found a man in that country that hired him to go into the fields and feed his hogs.

"One day, as the young man fed the hogs the husks of thrashed grain; he watched the animals rushing up to eat the dry, parched stubble he had thrown to them. While he watched them eating the meager meal, he was so hungry that the pigs' food looked good to him; for no one would give him even a bite to eat.

"Standing there watching them fighting over the scraps of grain, he finally came to his senses and said to himself, 'My father has lots of hired servants and they have plenty to eat and more; and here I am starving to death! I will go back home to my father and say to him; 'Father, I have sinned against you and against heaven. I am not worthy any more to be called your son, so just make me one of your servants.'

"He then left the pigs and started on his journey back to his father.

"Now when he was yet a far distance from his father's house, his father saw him coming up the road toward him. When his father saw him, he got tears in his eyes, felt deep compassion, and ran out to meet him. When he reached him, he embraced and kissed him, and smiled at him.

"But the son said, 'Father, I have sinned against heaven and against you, and I am no more worthy to be called your son.'

"The father, however, called for his servants, and when they came near, he said to them, 'Go to the house and get the best robe I have and put it on him; and put a ring on his finger and shoes on his feet. Go and kill the fatted calf, I have been saving in case he returned. Let us eat and be merry, for my son was dead, and is alive again. He was lost, but now he is found. They then went to the house and began rejoicing.

"Now the older son was in the fields; and when he neared the house, he heard music and dancing.

"As he reached the yard, he called to one of the servants and asked, 'What is all the music and dancing about?'

"The servant answered and said, 'Your brother has come home and your father has killed the fatted calf, because he has returned safe and sound.'

"But the older son was very angry and wouldn't go in. Therefore, the father came out, called for him and asked him why he was not coming in to celebrate with everyone.

"The young man answered, 'All these many years I have served you. I have never disobeyed you in anything you asked me to do; yet you never gave me even a young goat to cook so that I might have a party for my friends. But as soon as this son of yours has come home; the son that has wasted all his inheritance that you gave him on prostitutes, you kill the fatted calf for him and give him a party!'

"The father said, 'Son you are always with me, and all I have is yours. It is good that we are having a party and rejoicing; for your brother was dead and is alive again and was lost, but now is found.'

Chapter 24

A very tame fence lizard. Photo by author.

At Peace with the Animals

There is one story in this chapter that I have difficulty believing it happened, even though I was there and witnessed it myself. In fact, I was the one it happened to.

Before I get into that story, I will first mention that I have raised many animals over the years. Not only cats and dogs, but several wild animals: Opossums, groundhogs, rabbits, raccoons, and a few others

In early May of the year 2000, I found two orphaned raccoons in a tree in my yard. I named them Buddy and Rambo. Rambo got his name because he was so rambunctious. I videotaped them and they were on the national television program Real TV on December 7 of that same year. I also wrote a short book about them, which I mentioned earlier, that is still available on Amazon.

Buddy had a hind foot that had two toes fused together and it was easy to tell them apart. Buddy was also shyer than Rambo.

While the raccoons were growing up, they were free to come and go as they pleased. When they got older, they would come to the front porch each evening and want to be fed. One night, they came to the door and wanted a cookie, which was one of their favorite treats. As I was standing there handing them the cookies, I looked down and saw Rambo because his toes looked normal on his hind foot. I then looked over at the other raccoon and saw that it too had normal toes! *"One of these is a wild raccoon,"* I thought. It was then that the wild one took the cookie and walked off the porch to eat it, while Rambo stayed on the porch to eat his.

Another time, when I was feeding them, an opossum came onto the porch and wanted a cookie. He saw me feeding the raccoons and he wanted to be fed too. I tossed him one of the cookies and he sat on the porch and ate it.

Years later, I had two different female raccoons come to the house wanting to be fed and one even brought her young. They would take cookies from my hand and they were totally wild animals.

These things are amazing enough, but the real story is about another animal, a gray fox. What I'm about to tell you is true and I am not making it up, although many will believe that it could not have happened.

Now for the story that is hard to believe: Several years ago, we had at least two gray foxes coming to the house and eating cat food from our front porch. The food was for the two raccoons we were raising. We saw them often and I wondered what one would do if I caught it. Therefore, after locking the chickens and pigeons in their house, I put a screen door spring on the chicken coop door. Then tying a string to a stick, which held the door open, I ran it to a window in the house. I then put some scraps of meat on the ground leading to inside the pen.

Just before dark that evening, one of the foxes showed up. After finding the trail of meat, he proceeded to eat as he walked right into the coop. Pulling the string, the door quickly slammed shut behind the unsuspecting fox. Then, just as expected, the fox ran around the pen crashing into the wire trying to get out.

Rushing outside, I neared the pen expecting the fox to try even harder to get out, but to my surprise, he ran towards me, climbed the wire and sat on a limb I had put in the corner of the coop so my pigeons could perch there. I had heard of gray foxes climbing trees, but had never seen it myself. This was not the most surprising thing it did, however. Expecting the fox to go wild with fear as I approached, it instead sat there looking at me.

"This is incredible," I thought. *"Why doesn't it act afraid?"*

Then to my utter amazement, I took a piece of meat it had missed and putting it to the wire, the fox took it from my hand! I saw what was happening, but I still could not believe it. Calling my wife, Elizabeth, outside so she could be witness to this extraordinary event, she too fed the wild fox from her hand. If someone would have told me of this, I don't know if I would have believed them. It happened, I saw it, and I still have a hard time believing what I witnessed.

There is only one explanation I can give and that is a scripture from the Bible. Job 5:23 says, "For you will be in league with the stones of the field; and the beasts of the field will be at peace with you."

The fox must have sensed that I meant it no harm. Something similar happened one day at a neighbor's house. After I had visited a while, it was time to go home. As I was walking off the porch, I happened to look down to see a small fence lizard sunning itself on one of the steps. When I started going down the steps, the lizard did not run away or even move, but stayed still. Then reaching down, I stroked its back a couple of times. Finally, it moved from under foot and I continued on my way.

Both of these incidences made me feel close to God and I felt the animals knew this. That is the only reason I can think of why a wild fox would take food from my hand five minutes after being caught.

Yes, someday all animals will be at peace with humans. Until that day, however, animals will continue to die for good and for bad reasons.

`Epilogue

Above is the gorgeous Lady Amherst pheasant

When I was a young man, I loved hunting and fishing. It was a passion and I loved to be outdoors. I could not get enough of being in God's creation. As a small child, I loved baby animals as most children do. When I grew into a man, I still thought young animals were adorable but at the same I loved hunting, fishing, and bringing home the creatures I took from the wild. However, even as a child, I have compassion on animals and even if I killed them, I wanted them not to suffer. Some do not understand this. That is the reason for this book.

As I grew older, I learned that many animals that I loved to hunt are not good to eat by what God has said. Therefore, I quit eating them, and because I quit eating them, I quit hunting them.

In my younger days, I loved catching big catfish and frying them to a golden brown. I also loved fried frog legs, fried rabbit and others. I ate baked possum with sweet potatoes and barbequed raccoon.

I am now retired and can look back on my life. I am getting close to going the way that all of God's creatures go, and that is to turn back to dust. I can see things much more clearly now. Animals must die to supply our food and there is nothing wrong in killing them for such. Our world is in a place I wish it wasn't, and someday it will change. The Lord's Prayer tells us this, "Thy kingdom come, thy will be done on earth as it is in heaven." Someday the earth will be at peace and the lion *will* lie down beside the lamb. Until that day, however, we will have to wait.

After the Lord's kingdom comes, He will bring peace on the earth for a thousand years. When this is done, He will create a new heaven and a new earth. This is when all death the "last enemy," as God calls it, will be destroyed. Then, not only will animals never die, but also, we ourselves will have eternal life. We have that assurance from the one that made all things.

We now come to the end of the book. I hope I have made it clear that in many cases, it is not wrong to kill an animal and, in some cases, it is. We are in the final days of this world's system. Someday soon, man will nearly destroy himself and God will allow it. However, just before humans annihilate every living thing from the earth, including himself, God will intervene and stop the madness. Then there will be no more killing of anything. The wolf will lie down beside the lamb and a child will lead the beast from the wild. God will rule the entire earth and His knowledge will "be like the waters that covers the seas".

Until that day, however, we must eat, and as long as there is evil on the earth, other animals will be killed because of greed and selfishness. Everything is in God's hands and that is how we must look at it. In my younger days, it made me very sad to see the land where I used to roam destroyed by strip-mining and land development. It still saddens me somewhat, but I know that it must come to pass. It will also continue until man reaps what he has sown. He is already beginning to reap the reward of his shortsightedness, but there is much more to come. God made the earth and it is His. Today evil rules it, but this will soon change. We must do as the words on our money says, and it says, "In God we trust." That is all we can do. He is the only one that can help. We must do our best and then leave the rest up to Him.

The reason for this book is to answer the question is it wrong to kill animals. I believe by what God has said and what I have explained that it is not wrong, if you kill them for food (the ones that God has said were meant to be eaten). It is also not wrong, if they are killed for a purpose or good reason, if killed humanely. It is wrong, however, if they are rare, endangered, or if they are killed just for the sake of killing. It is even more wrong to be cruel to animals. It is much more human to kill an animal that to let it suffer or be cruel to it. If you have ever watched television westerns, as I did growing up in the fifties, a cowboy never let his horse suffer. When the cowboy's horse broke a leg, and was going to die a long agonizing death, he quickly put it out of its misery. He did this out of compassion, not cruelty.

There is one other Bible scripture that explains why animals must die as food for us and why they have been killed sometimes without much thought as to their importance. It is in Rom 8:19-22: "For the earnest expectation of the creature waits for the manifestation of the sons of God. For *the creature was made subject to vanity*, not willingly, but by reason of Him who hath subjected the same in hope, because *the creature itself also shall be delivered* from the *bondage of corruption* into the glorious liberty of the children of God. For we know that the whole creation groans and travails in pain together until now."

This explains very clearly that animals were put here to be eaten, not only by us, but also by other animals. It explains that their lives, right now, seem to be in vain, just to be born and die and abused sometimes. They were put under man's "care" and it shows that they are in pain, as we often are, about the condition of the world and the unfairness of death, disease, cruelty, and hardships. It also explains that this will end someday. It will end when God brings *His will* to the earth and then, not only will God's children be free from death, but so will all of creation.

There is one other Bible scripture that I wanted to include and it tells us how man has abused not only animals, but also the land. In the old book that I mentioned earlier, that was published in 1959 called *Wildlife in America* by Peter Matthiessen, there is a Bible quote that he has at the beginning of the book. It says, "And I brought you into a plentiful country, to eat the fruit thereof and the goodness thereof; but when you entered, you defiled my land, and made my heritage an abomination."—Jeremiah 2:7.

About the Author

Kenneth Edward Barnes has been called, *"A modern day Mark Twain"* by a local newspaper reporter for the first book he wrote titled *Life Along Little Pigeon Creek. "He shows a Twain sense of humor in conversation and in his writing. He writes in the 'down to earth' style that Twain used to capture the heart of America."*

He was born on April 4, 1951, along the banks of Little Pigeon Creek in the southern tip of Indiana, downstream from where Abraham Lincoln grew up. As a child, he loved fishing from the muddy banks of the creek and roaming in the nearby woods. He never missed an opportunity to be in the outdoors where he could see all of God's creation.

Ken is a nationally published writer, poet, and the author of over one hundred books. Some of his most popular ones are: *The Mammoth Slayers; A Cabin in the Woods; Mysteries of the Bible; Madam President; Life Along Little Pigeon Creek; A Book of Stories for Children; In Search of a Golden Sparrow; Buddy and Rambo: The Orphaned Raccoons; Outdoor Adventures; The Arkansas River Monster* collection, and *Do Pets go to Heaven?* This could soon change, however, as he has recently written several others.

The author became a member of *Hoosier Outdoor Writers* in 1993, where he has won several awards from them in their annual writing contest. He has also been a guest speaker for the *Boy Scouts, Daughters of the American Revolution, Teachers Reading Counsel, Kiwanis Club*, and at several schools, libraries, and churches.

Ken has been an outdoor columnist and contributing editor for several newspapers and magazines: *Ohio Valley Sportsman, Kentucky Woods and Waters, Southern Indiana Outdoors, Fur-Fish-Game, Wild Outdoor World, Mid-West Outdoors,* and a hard cover book titled *From the Field.* He has written for the *Boonville Standard, Perry County News, Newburgh Register and Chandler Post.* He has had poems published locally and nationally. One titled *The Stranger* went to missionaries around the world. The poem, *Princess,* was also published locally and nationally, and won honorable mention in a national contest. His best-loved poem is *Condemned* and has been published by the tens of thousands. Nearly every single poem he has written is in his colored paperback book, *Poems from the Heart,* and *My Favorite Poems.*

Ken has worked for an Evansville, Indiana, television station where he had outdoor news segments aired that he wrote, directed, and edited. He also had film clips that were aired on the national television shows *Real TV* and *Animal Planet.* At this time, he has several short videos on YouTube and on GodTube.

Studying nature since childhood, he is a self-taught ornithologist and a conservationist. In 2009, he became founder and president of the *Golden Sparrow Nature Society*, the name of which was chosen because of his first published book. Ken loves to share his knowledge and love of nature, and it has been said that he is a walking encyclopedia on birds and animals. Because of this, he recently published an E-book titled *Birds and Animals of Southern Indiana.* It has over 300 photos of birds and animals, most of which he photographed himself. He frequently updates it with new photos.

He has followed his dream of being a writer since 1978 and now lives in a cabin in the woods. Being an individualist, he cleared the land, dug a well by hand and built the house himself, which uses only solar electric. He even wrote a book titled *Solar Electric: How does that work?*

Comments or questions on the author's work can be left on his Facebook page at: **Kenneth Edward Barnes.** All of Ken's books can also be seen on his **Author Page** at Amazon.

Other Books by the Author

(My cabin in the woods)

Fictional Novels by
Kenneth Edward Barnes

1: The Mammoth Slayers
2: The Mammoth Slayers: Last Clan of Neanderthals
3: The Mammoth Slayers: The Last Neanderthal
4: The Mammoth Slayers: Rise of the Cro-Magnons
5: The Mammoth Slayers: The Final Chapter
6: The Mammoth Slayers: The Resurrection
7: The Mammoth Slayers: The Prequel
8: The Arkansas River Monster
9: Return of the Arkansas River Monster
10: The Capture of the Arkansas River Monster
11: The Last Arkansas River Monster
12: The Arkansas River Monster: The Complete Series
13: Into the West
14: The Black Widow
15: Betrayed

16: In Search of a Golden Sparrow
17: The Day That Time Stood Still
18: Madam President
19: To Keep a Secret
20: Ransom

Non-fiction Novels

21: Life Along Little Pigeon Creek
22: The Long Pond Road
23: A Cabin in the Woods
24: Barnestorming the Outdoors: Revised Edition
25: Kenneth Edward Barnes: An Autobiography
26: Saving Wildlife

Novels and Novelettes for Children

27: The Invasion of the Dregs
28: The Creature of O'Minee
29: Kenny's Children's Stories (unpublished)
30: A Book of Stories for Children
31: Plays for Children
32: Buddy and Rambo: The Orphaned Raccoons

Books of Faith

33: A Biblical Mystery: Christians need to become a Jew: What does this mean?
34: A Day Appointed
35: A House Divided: This is why Donald Trump won the election
36: A Rude Awakening
37: Abortion: Why all the controversy?
38: Beyond the Grave: Is there life after death?
39: Bible Secrets Revealed
40: Christ: His Words, His Life

Books Available as E-books only

75: Birds and Animals of Southern Indiana
76: The Ancient Art of Falconry
77. There a Devil? Is Satan Real?
78: The Thirteenth Disciple
79: The Two Witnesses
80: Solar Electric: How does that work?